KING CHARLES III

A LIFE STORY

Sally Morgan

Illustrated by Sarah Papworth

■ SCHOLASTIC

Published in the UK by Scholastic, 2023
1 London Bridge, London, SE1 9BG
Scholastic Ireland, 89E Lagan Road, Dublin Industrial Estate, Glasnevin,
Dublin, D11 HP5F

SCHOLASTIC and associated logos are trademarks and/or
registered trademarks of Scholastic Inc.

Text © Sally Morgan, 2023
Illustrations by Sarah Papworth © Scholastic, 2023

ISBN 978 07023 2865 7

Printed by CPI Group (UK) Ltd, Croydon, CR0 4YY
Paper made from wood grown in sustainable forests
and other controlled sources.

1 3 5 7 9 10 8 6 4 2

www.scholastic.co.uk

CONTENTS

THE KING'S FIRST STEPS

On 13 December 2022, King Charles III stood in front of a television camera at St George's Chapel, Windsor Castle, to deliver a very important message. It would soon be Charles's seventy-fourth Christmas, but it would be his first without his mother, Queen Elizabeth II, and his first as king. This meant it was the first Christmas that he would be expected to record an address to be broadcast to the nation on Christmas Day.

A Royal Tradition

The first royal Christmas message was read by Charles's great-grandfather King George V in 1932. The first Christmas message was written by Rudyard Kipling, the author of *The Jungle Book*, and was broadcast live at 3.00 pm from the king's estate at Sandringham (see page 46).

"THROUGH ONE OF THE MARVELS OF MODERN SCIENCE, I AM ENABLED, THIS CHRISTMAS DAY, TO SPEAK TO ALL MY PEOPLES THROUGHOUT THE EMPIRE."

King George V

As well as to the United Kingdom, the king's message was broadcast on radio stations across the globe. The speech was meant to be a one-time event, but proved so popular that it became a tradition for the monarch to speak to people at Christmas and give his or her best wishes from his or her home.

The tradition was continued by his son, King George VI, followed by his granddaughter Queen Elizabeth II twenty-five years after his very first speech. When the tradition fell to Queen Elizabeth II the 'marvels of modern science' had moved on. The invention of television meant that as well as being able to hear the sovereign in their homes they could see her, too.

Throughout her reign, Queen Elizabeth delivered a Christmas message almost every year. When she delivered her message in 2021, nobody knew that this would be her last. In her message, Elizabeth spoke about how Christmas, though a happy time for many people, could be a difficult time for those who had lost people who were close to them. Elizabeth empathized with these people because she was one of them, having lost her husband, Prince Philip, earlier in the year. Elizabeth used her speech to express her gratitude for all the messages of love and support she had received since he died.

"LIFE, OF COURSE, CONSISTS OF FINAL PARTINGS AS WELL AS FIRST MEETINGS."

Queen Elizabeth II, 2021

Elizabeth paid tribute to Philip for his years of service, his work with young people and for his being an 'early champion' of environmental causes – work that had been shared and amplified by her son Prince Charles and her grandson Prince William.

Elizabeth looked forward to the year ahead, particularly to her Platinum Jubilee celebrations, which would begin in the following February.

Elizabeth said her jubilee would be a chance for everyone to reflect on the many changes that had taken place during the seventy years since she came to the throne, and while this was true, there was another change on the horizon.

Sadly, Elizabeth's health did not allow her to take part in many of her celebrations, but just as he had taken on his father's work, Charles now stepped in for his mother, performing many of her official obligations for the year.

QUEEN ELIZABETH II – THE LONGEST REIGNING MONARCH IN BRITISH HISTORY

Queen Elizabeth II was born in 1926, to Prince Albert, Duke of York, and his wife Elizabeth, Duchess of York. Elizabeth's father became king, taking the name George VI, when she was ten years old. This made the young Princess Elizabeth heir to the throne.

In 1947, Princess Elizabeth married a man named Philip, born a prince of Greece and Denmark, but who renounced these titles to marry Elizabeth and become Duke of Edinburgh. Elizabeth and Philip's marriage lasted seventy-three years, until Philip's death in 2021. Elizabeth and Philip had four children together: Charles, Anne, Andrew and Edward.

King George VI was a popular king, but he became unwell. As heir, Elizabeth took on many of his official duties, including his royal tours. In 1952, while on her way to tour Australia and New Zealand, Elizabeth was given the message that her father had died and that she was queen.

Queen Elizabeth reigned for 70 years and 214 days, longer than any other king or queen of the United Kingdom. Seven years longer than her nearest rival, her great-great-grandmother Queen

Victoria. During her reign, Elizabeth carried out more than 20,000 public engagements, visited 117 countries, posed for more than one hundred official portraits, and worked with fifteen prime ministers of the United Kingdom. Elizabeth met with her last prime minister, Elizabeth Truss, on 6 September 2022.

Elizabeth died aged ninety-six, at her home, Balmoral Castle, on 8 September 2022, surrounded by members of her family including her son Charles.

The funeral of Queen Elizabeth II took place on 19 September 2022 at Westminster Abbey, followed by a service at St George's Chapel, Windsor, where she was laid to rest beside her beloved husband, Prince Philip, Duke of Edinburgh.

Charles paid tribute to his mother's life of service, and just as she had done in her last speech, thanked people for all of the kind messages of support he had received since her death.

A Momentous Year

Looking back, the year 2022 had been perhaps the most momentous of Charles's life. At the moment of his mother's death, Charles became king. At an age at which most people would be considering retiring from work if they had not done so already, Charles had a new job and was busier than ever. Charles had to put his grief aside and start work right away, first leading the nation in mourning and then performing a long list of the duties he had watched his mother perform since he was a little boy. It was a challenging time for Charles, and it was a challenging time for the country.

In his Christmas address, Charles said that he and his mother shared a belief that all people had within them the power to do good and serve people in need. Charles thanked people who had served their community or contributed to society by donating money or volunteering when so many people around the country were struggling to pay their bills.

"I PARTICULARLY WANT TO PAY TRIBUTE TO ALL THOSE WONDERFULLY KIND PEOPLE WHO SO GENEROUSLY GIVE FOOD OR DONATIONS, OR THE MOST PRECIOUS COMMODITY OF ALL, THEIR TIME, TO SUPPORT THOSE AROUND THEM IN GREATEST NEED."

King Charles III, 2023

One of the needs Charles was referring to was the fact that many people around the country were struggling to pay their bills due to the cost of living crisis.

COST OF LIVING CRISIS

The prices of the things you see in shops go up all the time. This is due to something called inflation. Inflation measures how much more something cost this year compared to how much it would have cost the year before. While prices go up almost every year, in the year 2022, almost everything in the United Kingdom was much more expensive than it had been the year before due to a high rate of inflation. While inflation made everything more expensive, people's salaries and the amount of money people received from the government in the form of benefits, often stayed the same. This meant that it became more difficult for people to afford to buy the things they were able to the year before. If people found it hard to pay for all of their living expenses such as food, energy (gas and electricity), taxes, transport and accommodation (rent or mortgage payments), it would be harder if not impossible for them to do so in 2022.

Charities across the country had already been providing food banks where people in need could come to access food. In response to the crisis, these charities supported even more people, and local communities opened up buildings where people could keep warm.

What a State!

Although King Charles had only been king for three months, he had already held audiences with two different prime ministers. Liz Truss had become Prime Minister after her predecessor Prime Minister Boris Johnson resigned. Following his resignation, the party he represented, known as the Conservative Party, held a series of votes to decide who should be their next leader, and lead the country. On 5 September, Liz Truss won the vote and was invited to meet Queen Elizabeth at Balmoral the very next day.

But she wasn't prime minister for very long. The policies Prime Minister Liz Truss implemented while in power were unpopular, and had some disastrous consequences including making the British pound worth less than it had been in many years. After just six weeks, the shortest term of any British prime minister, Liz Truss resigned.

First Kissing

As head of state, the duty fell to Charles to invite the person voted by the Conservative Party as leader, Rishi Sunak, to form a government. On 25 October, King Charles III invited Rishi Sunak to Buckingham Palace for an important ceremony known as the 'kissing of hands.' In the past, prime ministers were expected to kneel before the sovereign before kissing their hands as a symbolic act of their loyalty. Today, although the ceremony retains the name, a new prime minister is expected only to shake the offered hand.

Rishi Sunak

Despite the lack of actual kissing, it was a ceremony of firsts, for Charles, the prime minister and for the country. For Charles it was the first time he had invited a prime minister to form a government in his name. For Rishi Sunak it was his first audience with King Charles, and first day as prime minister. For the United Kingdom, Prime Minister Rishi Sunak was the first South Asian and first Hindu ever to be appointed to the highest office in the land.

A New Reign

But while many of the sentiments in Charles's message were similar to those of his mother and even his grandfather, it was still a message that reflected who he was as king and who he had been as Prince of Wales.

Charles delivered his speech in front of a Christmas tree decorated in sustainable decorations made from glass and paper as well as natural pine cones. As Prince of Wales, Charles was one of the first voices who spoke on the importance of preserving the environment, and working towards living sustainably.

Charles also paid tribute to the contribution made by people of all faiths to the country and acknowledged those who had no faith at all.

After recording his message, Charles spent his Christmas at Sandringham Estate in Norfolk, with his wife, Queen Consort Camilla, by his side.

CAMILLA, QUEEN CONSORT – A NEW AND NOBLE QUEEN

Camilla was born Camilla Rosemary Shand in London on 17 July 1947. Camilla's grandfather was a baron, a title which he inherited from his father. This meant that Camilla was a member of a part of society called 'the nobility'. The nobility is made up of the families of people with inherited titles, such as dukes, earls, marquesses and barons. The rest of the population of the United Kingdom are known as 'commoners'.

Growing up, Camilla moved between two large homes, one set in the countryside in East Sussex and the other in South Kensington, one of London's most expensive districts.

In 1973, Camilla Rosemary Shand married an army lieutenant named Andrew Parker Bowles. Camilla and Andrew had two children together, but divorced in 1995.

On 8 April 2005, Camilla married Charles, then Prince of Wales. After her marriage, Camilla became the Princess of Wales, but instead went by the title of Duchess of Cornwall.

As Duchess of Cornwall, Camilla represented and worked with over one hundred charities serving a diverse mix of causes such as the survivors of domestic abuse and people living with diseases, such as osteoporosis (a disease that causes your bones to weaken and more likely to break) to The Royal School of Needlework.

With his first steps as king behind him, many wondered what Charles's life had been like and what the reign of King Charles III and Queen Consort Camilla would mean, not only for the monarchy, but for the United Kingdom, and the world.

Charles waving at first engagement as king

A BABY AT
BUCKINGHAM PALACE

At 9.14 pm on 14 November 1948 a baby was born in Westminster, London, but not in a hospital as you might expect. This baby was born on the first floor of Buckingham Palace. Outside, a crowd gathered eager to hear news of the birth, because this baby was no ordinary baby: he was a prince. This baby was born to Princess Elizabeth and Prince Philip, and while all parents look at their babies and hope they grow up to have a bright and exciting future ahead of them, Princess Elizabeth and Prince Philip knew that their baby could look forward to a future very different to that of any other child in the country – in fact, any other child in the world – because one day, this baby would be king.

Shortly after the birth, the post office located in the palace got to work sending telegrams to British ambassadors and foreign leaders around the world. The crowd outside the palace was not forgotten; a palace official walked to the gate and posted this formal bulletin.

"Her Royal Highness the Princess Elizabeth was safely delivered of a prince at 9.14 o'clock this evening. Her Royal Highness and the infant prince are both well."

The crowd erupted in a mighty cheer which went on for so long and was so loud that after a few hours the police drove through the gathered revellers delivering a message from the palace to keep the noise down so that the princess and the infant prince could get some rest. "Ladies and gentleman, it is requested from the palace that we have a little quietness, if you please."

Celebrations were held all around London in honour of the prince's birth and the fountains in Trafalgar Square were lit up blue in his honour. As the news spread, parties were held around the country and the next morning churches everywhere rang their bells in celebration.

LONDON IN 1948

The London that this baby boy was born into looked a bit different from the London you might see today. Prince Charles was born just three years after the end of a major world conflict known as the Second World War. The Second World War lasted from 1939 to 1945. During the war, the German air force, known as the *Luftwaffe*, dropped bombs on major cities and military targets around Great Britain. This became known as 'the Blitz'. London, like other major cities such as Liverpool, Coventry and Glasgow, still bore the scars of the bombings that took place during the Blitz. London's streets were filled with smashed-up buildings that had not yet been rebuilt. Buckingham Palace itself was bombed in September 1940 and had yet to be repaired.

As news spread of the little prince's birth, congratulations from people around the world flooded in. These congratulations came from world leaders as well as ordinary people. Well-wishers sent so many cards and gifts that the palace set up a special department to deal with it all and reply to the correspondence.

Right Royal Parents

Princess Elizabeth was the daughter of King George VI. When Princess Elizabeth was born to the then Duke and Duchess of York, nobody thought that she would one day be queen. This was because her father, the Duke of York, had an older brother, Edward, Prince of Wales. As the king's eldest son, the Prince of Wales was heir to the throne. When George V died in 1936, Edward was proclaimed King Edward VIII. However, the reign of King Edward VIII lasted less than a year. Shortly after becoming king, Edward said

King George VI

he wished to marry an American woman named Wallis Simpson. But there was a problem: Wallis Simpson had been married twice before.

This was a problem because as king, Edward's decision on who to marry was not just his own. Whoever Edward chose to marry had to be approved by the Church of England, and by the British government. The Church of England did not allow divorced people to remarry in a church until 2002 and the government did not approve of the match. The government gave Edward an ultimatum: he could either keep his throne or his fiancée. Edward chose his fiancée and on 11 December 1936, less than one year after he was proclaimed king, Edward VIII took to the airwaves to announce that he was stepping down, or abdicating the throne, in favour of his brother Albert, who was proclaimed King George VI the very next day, making Princess Elizabeth the future Queen of the United Kingdom.

PRINCE PHILIP, DUKE OF EDINBURGH

Prince Philip was a first lieutenant in the Royal Navy who had served in the Second World War; he was also a member of the Greek and Danish Royal Families. Prince Philip met Princess Elizabeth in 1939, when he showed her family around the naval college at Dartmouth where he was studying. Elizabeth was just thirteen years old at the time, but the pair kept in touch, and on 20 November 1947 they married at Westminster Abbey. Being in the Royal Navy, Prince Philip was often called to be away at sea, but for a while after he was married he settled down in London and worked at the Admiralty and at the naval college in Greenwich.

While in some ways, this baby was unlike other babies, there were many ways in which he was just like them. For one, the baby prince would need somewhere to sleep. The palace had just the thing – a crib, lined with pink satin and lace, used by his mother when she was born. This crib was placed in the dressing room next to Princess Elizabeth's bedroom on the second floor of the palace. Like other babies, the baby prince would need someone to take care of him when his mother and father were busy or resting. For this the little prince had not one, but two specially trained nannies – Nanny Lightbody and Nanny Anderson. These nannies were in charge of looking after the little prince and taking him out of the palace to get some fresh air in the gardens or to Green Park. They were also two of the few people apart from close family who saw the little prince for the first weeks of his life. This was because Princess Elizabeth and Prince Philip wanted to keep the prince to themselves for as long as possible and to maintain their privacy while Princess Elizabeth recovered from the birth.

In Great Britain, many people were eagerly awaiting pictures and news about the royal baby and newspapers published stories speculating what the young couple would name their son.

Stories about the royal baby referred to him as the infant prince and people were getting impatient to know more. One of the reasons people were so interested in hearing about the young prince was because it was happy news. Life for many people in the United Kingdom was hard in 1948 and stories about a young couple celebrating the birth of a new baby was an interesting change from headlines about food shortages and power cuts.

THE UNITED KINGDOM IN 1948

Just like in London, all around the United Kingdom, everywhere was feeling the effects of the Second World War. After the war, the British pound wasn't worth as much as it had been before the war, which meant buying food from other counties was very expensive. This led to food shortages. To make sure everyone was able to get enough to eat, the government continued a system used during the war called rationing, which limited the amount of foods such as meat, eggs, flour and sugar people were allowed to buy in shops.

Fuel from abroad was also very expensive. Coal shortages meant people couldn't afford to heat their homes and often there wasn't enough coal to fuel the power stations to make electricity. Without the coal to power them, some power stations had to shut. Despite record-breaking cold weather in the winter of 1946-47, people were only allowed to use their electricity for a few hours during the day.

The reason the United Kingdom could not grow more food or dig up more of its own coal was because the war had caused a shortage of workers. Many men died during the war and many more were injured so badly they were no longer able to work. Not only this, but many people who did these jobs during the war were old and had delayed their retirement until the war was over. Workers were needed more than ever. As well as miners and farm workers, builders were needed to repair bombed buildings, healthcare workers were needed in hospitals, and the country was short of factory workers and train and bus drivers. Thankfully, help to rebuild the country was on the way. The British government appealed to the empire (see page 53) for help. In June 1948, five months before Charles was born, the first ship named HMT *Empire Windrush* arrived with 539 people from the Caribbean island of Jamaica on board. These were the first of many people invited by the government to fill vital jobs in factories, healthcare and public transport.

HMT Empire Windrush ship

The Prince Makes a Name for Himself

Princess Elizabeth and Prince Philip had chosen to name their son Charles Philip Arthur George, but kept this to themselves. The rest of the world had to wait until the young prince's christening, almost a month after he was born, to find out.

On 15 December 1948, the young prince was dressed in an ivory satin gown and taken to the music room of Buckingham Palace for his christening. Normally, a religious ceremony like this would have taken place in the palace chapel, but the chapel had been badly damaged when Buckingham Palace was bombed in 1940 and had not yet been repaired.

A christening is a religious ceremony in which a person is welcomed into the Christian faith. During a christening, a religious minister sprinkles water on the head of the child being christened. The water used in a christening ceremony is known as holy water and has been blessed by a church official.

While children's christenings are an important event for any Christian family, Prince Charles's christening was significant because, as a future king he would one day be the Supreme Governor of the Church of England, or Anglican Church.

To help Prince Charles prepare for his future, he would need guidance, and at his christening he was given what are known as "godparents". A godparent is a person chosen by a child's parents to act as a religious advisor to the child as they are growing up. While most children who have been christened have two, three or four godparents, Charles was given eight.

NO ORDINARY CHRISTENING

As well as getting more than the average number of godparents, there were other things about Charles's christening that were a bit different from other Christian children's ceremonies.

The font – In a christening, a font is the bowl containing the holy water sprinkled on the baby's head. The font used at Prince Charles's christening is called the Lily Font. It is made of pure silver covered in gold and was designed by Queen Victoria and her husband Prince Albert in 1840 for the christening of their first child.

The water – The water in the font was taken from the River Jordan and blessed by the archbishop of Canterbury.

The gown – The long ivory dress worn by the prince is known as the Honiton Lace Gown. The Honiton Lace Gown was made for the eldest daughter of Queen Victoria, Princess Victoria, and was used for every royal christening after, until a replica gown was commissioned by Queen Elizabeth II in 2004. The replica gown was used for the christenings of Prince George, Princess Charlotte and Prince Louis, and Prince Harry's son Archie.

After the ceremony, Prince Charles Philip Arthur George's name was revealed to the public alongside pictures of him with his mother, father and the rest of his family.

Baby Charles with his parents and grandparents on his christening

An Ailing King

The pictures of the christening show a happy, smiling family, but all was not well. Prince Charles's grandfather, King George VI, was suffering from health problems. For a while, the king thought he only had a bad cough, but it would turn out to be something much more serious.

Normally, the royal family travelled to one of their homes in the countryside to celebrate Christmas, but in 1948, the palace doctors advised the king to stay in London for treatment, so Prince Charles spent his first Christmas at Buckingham Palace.

ON THE MOVE

When Elizabeth and Philip married, they were given a large house in London named Clarence House, but they couldn't move in right away. Clarence House, like many big houses at the time, had been put to use in the war. Clarence House had been converted into offices for the Red Cross (a charity). Before Princess Elizabeth, Prince Philip and Prince Charles could move in it had to be made into a home again. Until the work was complete, they lived at Buckingham Palace with the king and queen.

Clarence House

By July 1949, when Charles was just over seven months old, Clarence House was ready. It was now a beautiful home. Clarence House is just half a mile away from Buckingham Palace. To make sure Charles wasn't too disrupted by the change, he took some of his favourite toys with him including a fluffy, blue elephant named Jumbo. Charles's nannies also moved with him, and so his life went on very much as it had before.

A DAY IN THE LIFE OF A LITTLE PRINCE

7 am Curtains opened. Wash, dress and eat breakfast with his nannies in the nursery.

9 am Time with Mummy, Princess Elizabeth. Usually thirty minutes to an hour.

9.30 am Back to the nursery to play. Yay! Jumbo!

10.30 am Out for a walk in the pram with Nanny Lightbody or Nanny Anderson as well as a plain-clothed personal protection police officer.

1.00 pm Lunch! Boiled chicken and rice. Yum!

2.00 pm Nap or rest time. Zzzzzz.

3.00 pm Perhaps a trip out? Off to Marlborough House to see Gan-gan's house and play with her fancy figurines!

4.00 pm Back to the nursery for tea!

6.00 pm Bath and bedtime in the nursery with Mummy and nanny.

7.00 pm Story, prayers and sleep. Zzzzzz.

While Charles's life might look a little odd, rich families often employed nannies to live with the family to look after their children's day-to-day needs until they were old enough to be sent to school. Charles loved his nannies and because he spent so much time with them, when he said his first word when he was around a year old, it was "Nana".

Gan-Gan's House

As well as his parents and nannies, Prince Charles grew up with lots of family around him. Not only were his grandparents King George VI and Queen Elizabeth just down the road at Buckingham Palace, his great-grandmother, Queen Mary, lived a short walk away at Marlborough House. Queen Mary adored spending time with her great-grandson. When Charles first learned to talk, he struggled to say Great-grandmother, so he called Queen Mary Gan-Gan – a nickname that stuck.

Queen Mary of Teck

Queen Mary had been Queen of the United Kingdom and the British Dominions and Empress of India from 6 May 1910 to 29 January 1936. As queen consort, Mary supported her husband King George V in his role as sovereign until his death in 1936.

Queen Mary had six children, including King

Edward VIII and King George VI (Charles's grandfather). According to her children, Queen Mary had been a strict and exacting mother, but as a great-grandmother, Queen Mary was warm and indulgent, allowing Charles to climb up into her lap and play with her precious jade ornaments which had been off-limits to her own children.

Hardworking Parents

As the eldest daughter of King George VI, Elizabeth had many duties including attending public events and meeting with the charities of which she was patron. As a patron, Elizabeth supported organizations by using her fame and influence to draw attention to the charities' work and the people they served.

As well as her own work as a princess, Elizabeth was also expected to take on some of her father's duties. George VI had been unwell for some time, making some of his duties as king difficult for him. As King George's health worsened Elizabeth was expected to be away from home more and more.

Charles's father, Prince Philip, was an officer in the Royal Navy who had served in the Second World War. Philip was often away at sea on duty in the Mediterranean, which made it hard for him to spend time with his wife and new family. Elizabeth flew out to be with him whenever she could.

Elizabeth and Philip

Charles's First Christmas at Sandringham

Just before Christmas 1949, Elizabeth flew to spend the holiday with Philip and enjoy some warm weather. Elizabeth left Charles in the care of her mother and father as well as his two nannies, and while he might have missed his mother, he had plenty to look forward to. Charles

43

travelled to Sandringham to spend Christmas with his grandparents.

SANDRINGHAM HOUSE – A FAMILY HOME

Sandringham Estate in Norfolk was bought by Charles's great-great-grandfather, King Edward VII, in 1862. Sandringham is located about 100 miles from London and is set in 20,000 acres of countryside. There is a working farm on the estate. Sandringham was a special place for King George VI because he was born there and enjoyed spending time in the countryside and out of public view.

Two of King George VI's favourite things were spending time with his family and being at Sandringham, and so at Christmas it became a tradition for the royal family to travel from their various homes to spend Christmas together there.

Christmas at Sandringham

Just like any family, the royal family had holiday traditions which began long before December. Charles's grandmother, Elizabeth, liked to make a start on the Christmas pudding on the last Sunday in November known as 'stir it up Sunday' using a seventeenth century family recipe.

The staff at Sandringham cut mistletoe and holly from the estate and decorated the house. Closer to the big day, the family helped decorate a twenty-foot Christmas tree with ornaments. Charles was too young to be much help, but his cousins were happy to step in. They also helped to display hundreds of Christmas cards sent by well-wishers around the world, covering every surface they could find.

Thankfully, Charles didn't have to wait too long to open his presents. The family attended a service at St Mary Magdalene Church on Christmas morning, so they got to open their presents on Christmas Eve.

You might think that a little prince would get more presents than he would know what to do with, but although Prince Charles and members of the royal family were often sent thousands of presents from people all over the world, there are very strict rules on which gifts they are allowed to accept. Generally, royal family members are only allowed to accept gifts from family members or good friends. It wouldn't be long until Charles got someone to share his presents and his nursery with.

On Christmas day, the family went to church in the morning before coming home to eat Christmas lunch. At some point, King George VI left the family to go to his study which had been transformed into a radio studio. In his study, the king read a speech to wish everyone in Great Britain and around the empire and commonwealth a happy Christmas.

A Little Princess

On 15 August 1950, Prince Charles got a new playmate in the nursery at Clarence House, a little sister named Anne Elizabeth Alice Louise.

On the same day Charles's sister was born, the family got other important news. Philip received word that he was to be given command of his first ship, HMS *Magpie* in the Mediterranean. Soon after Anne was born, Philip left to go to sea.

While Charles was at home with his sister, his life followed its normal routine, but there was no escaping the fact that Charles and Anne weren't ordinary children. One example of this was that on their daily walks Charles started to notice how people would stare at them and photographers would try to get pictures of them. To avoid this, the nannies would take the children to parks further and further away from home for their walks in the hope that they would go unnoticed.

Daddy Comes Home

In 1951, King George VI's health took a turn

for the worse and the few duties he had been able to perform the previous year would now be impossible for him. Not only this, the palace doctors had informed him that he needed surgery which, even if it were successful, would take a long time to recover from.

As heir to the throne, Elizabeth had no choice but to take on more and more of her father's obligations at home and abroad. She needed help. Philip made the difficult decision to leave his command and return home to Clarence House in July 1951.

But Elizabeth and Philip weren't home for very long. Shortly before Charles's third birthday, in October 1951 his mother and father set off on a tour of Canada and the USA.

Charles spent his third birthday at Buckingham Palace with his grandparents and his aunt Princess Margaret. Although Charles did not spend his birthday with his parents, he was far from lonely. His grandmother, Queen Elizabeth, was devoted to him and spent as much time with him as she could.

"SHE WAS QUITE SIMPLY THE MOST MAGICAL GRANDMOTHER YOU COULD POSSIBLY HAVE."

King Charles III

Charles's favourite of his two nannies was Mabel Anderson. Mabel could see that Charles was a shy boy. She knew he was going to grow up to have a very public life. Mabel was gentle with Charles and taught him important lessons to help him overcome his shyness, such as looking people in the eye when he was talking to them and not to pull unhappy faces.

A Family Christmas

Charles's mother and father were home in time to celebrate Christmas with the family at

Sandringham. Charles was happy to see them but was disappointed when he discovered they would soon have to leave to go on a tour, in place of the king, of the commonwealth that included Australia and New Zealand.

WHAT IS THE COMMONWEALTH?

The king or queen of Great Britain is also the head of something called the Commonwealth of Nations. The Commonwealth of Nations was set up in 1931, for the countries that were once part of the British Empire, who now govern themselves but choose to maintain a relationship with Britain and each other. Rather than be ruled by Britain, these countries form an alliance of independent and equal nations. Some countries have since chosen to leave the commonwealth, while others with no ties to the old British Empire have chosen to join.

During his Christmas speech, King George VI said how sorry he was not to be able to travel:

"IT HAS BEEN A GREAT
DISAPPOINTMENT TO THE
QUEEN AND TO MYSELF THAT
WE HAVE BEEN COMPELLED
TO GIVE UP FOR THE SECOND
TIME THE TOUR WHICH WE
HAD PLANNED FOR NEXT
YEAR. WE WERE LOOKING
FORWARD TO MEETING MY
PEOPLES IN THEIR OWN
HOMES AND WE REALIZE
THAT THEY WILL SHARE OUR
REGRET THAT THIS CANNOT

BE. I AM VERY GLAD THAT OUR DAUGHTER, PRINCESS ELIZABETH, WITH HER HUSBAND, WILL BE ABLE TO VISIT THESE COUNTRIES AND I KNOW THAT THEIR WELCOME THERE WILL BE AS WARM AS THAT WHICH AWAITED US."

King George VI

In his speech, the king offered words of encouragement for people who were far away and thinking of their families at home saying that the people of Great Britain were, "a home-loving people, but we have never been a 'stay at home' people."

THE BRITISH EMPIRE

The people of Great Britain were not a 'stay-at-home' people. From the late 1500s England and other European countries such as Spain, sent ships filled with people around the world to claim the lands as territory belonging to their kings and queens, even though people already lived there. The people on board these ships were called settlers and these settlers set up what were known as colonies. By the 1880s, thirty per cent of the continent of Africa was under British rule and by 1913 the British Empire covered one third of the Earth's surface and was home to over 400 million people.

People in Great Britain were told that the people who already lived in these countries were primitive and uncivilized, and that one of the most important duties of the British people was to build an empire to bring other countries the 'benefits' of British civilization such as the

British justice system and religion. In return, the British ransacked these people's history and exported their sacred treasures to fill museums and grand houses. They dug up their land to extract resources such as gemstones and precious metals. They cut down their forests to plant vast plantations of rubber, palm oil and tea. Between 1663 and the late 1880s they imprisoned and trafficked enslaved people to work in lands far from where they were born.

The British built roads and railways in order to transport these goods and people to the ports so they could be shipped and sold around the world. Much of the money from the sale of these goods went to British companies and was paid to the British government in taxes. Relatively little of the money went to the people who worked on the land and who had called the area home for thousands of years.

From the beginning, people in these countries resisted British rule, but Great Britain used the money raised from these territories to fund a vast army and navy to crush their rebellions – but this was expensive. Some countries who fought the British won their independence, such as the United States of America in 1776.

In the 1900s, because of the First World War, the British government found that it did not have enough money to maintain control of these countries, and as more countries demanded their independence, they were granted dominion status. A dominion is a country which is still a part of the empire but is allowed to govern itself, set its own laws and elect its own leaders.

After the Second World War, Great Britain had even less money to maintain its empire and many people in Britain no longer supported the idea that the British had the right to rule countries overseas. As more countries fought against British rule, more won independence.

After celebrating Christmas with the family at Sandringham, Elizabeth and Philip set off on their tour of the commonwealth on 31 January 1952. The tour which began in Kenya was supposed to last many months, but they were needed at home much sooner than anyone expected.

SAYING GOODBYE

On 6 February 1952, Charles woke and ate his breakfast in his bedroom, just as he did every morning, but it wasn't long before he realized that something was very wrong. The first thing Charles noticed was that he and Anne weren't taken to his grandmother's room at the usual time. In fact, they were left in the nursery for most of the morning. The next thing Charles noticed was that when he and Anne did eventually leave the nursery, the staff around the house looked sad or were crying. Curious, Charles asked Nanny Lightbody what was happening. Nanny Lightbody told Charles that his grandfather, King George VI, had gone away. Charles was confused; usually when his grandfather went away he made it a point to say goodbye, and even though the staff liked his grandfather very much, they didn't go about crying every time he went on a trip. Unsatisfied, Charles asked to speak to his grandmother but was told he would have to wait.

When his grandmother did come, she told Charles that his mother and father would be home much sooner than expected. This confused Charles even more. He knew how carefully planned these trips were and that, if they were coming home early, something must be very wrong. Impatient to know what was happening, Charles asked his grandmother why his grandfather had left without saying goodbye. She looked at her confused grandson and burst into tears.

A Funeral Fit for A King

It wasn't long before Charles and the rest of the country found out that King George VI had died. Charles's mother was flying home, not only to be with her family, but because she was now Queen Elizabeth II.

Charles had always been very close to his grandfather and missed him very much. Thankfully, he had his nannies to comfort him in his grief. Soon his mother would be home too.

But as queen, his mother would be busier than ever before, and Charles's world would never be the same.

When someone dies, it is a tradition in most families to hold some kind of a funeral or farewell to give people a chance to say goodbye. The same is true for the royal family, with one big difference. King George VI was a husband, a father and a grandfather but he was also a king, which meant that instead of a small funeral attended by family and friends, his was a State funeral, which is a national event attended by thousands of people.

From Sandringham, King George VI's coffin was taken to Westminster Hall in London. There, it was displayed on a platform called a catafalque. People who wished to pay their respects were invited to line up outside the hall for their chance to pass by the coffin. More than 300,000 people came. The king's funeral was held on 15 February and attended by the royal family, members of parliament and leaders from around the world. Many more thousands of people from all over the country travelled to see the funeral procession.

Prince Charles was not among them. Charles's mother and father felt that such a big occasion would be too much for a three-year-old boy. Instead, Charles and Anne stayed at Sandringham under the care of their nannies.

A New Old Home

As well as keeping Charles and Anne from the funeral, Queen Elizabeth and Prince Philip did what they could to maintain Charles and Anne's routine, but there was no escaping from the fact that their lives were going to change.

The first change was a change of address. Charles and Anne spent their Easter holiday with their family at Windsor Castle. But instead of returning to Clarence House, Charles and Anne were driven to their new home – Buckingham Palace.

The queen had arranged for the nursery in Buckingham Palace to be decorated in the same colours as the nursery in Clarence House and for all their favourite toys to be there when they arrived. For Charles, this was his Tudor dolls' house and an enormous collection of tin soldiers.

Buckingham Palace was not an ideal home for a family. Not only was it vast, with hundreds of rooms, it was also a place of work, teeming with offices and administrators, and while it may have Charles's set of toy soldiers, there was a host of real ones, with loaded guns, marching up and down outside.

BUCKINGHAM PALACE

Buckingham Palace has been the London home of the kings and queens of the United Kingdom since 1837. The palace has 775 rooms, 52 royal and guest bedrooms and 188 bedrooms for staff who work within the palace. As well as being a home, Buckingham Palace also contains 92 offices devoted to organizing the lives of the royal family. Buckingham Palace has 19 state rooms in which the monarch performs his or her duties. Every year, Buckingham Palace is the venue for state occasions, such as banquets and balls, as well as meetings called audiences. Buckingham Palace was opened to the public in 1993 and attracts millions of visitors each year.

Buckingham Palace is owned by the Crown Estate. Properties that are part of the Crown Estate belong to the king or queen only for the duration of their reign and cannot be sold by them. Profits from the Crown Estate from rent, entrance fees or other means go to HM Treasury, the part of the government that deals with finance and public spending. Sandringham House and Balmoral Castle are private homes and can be sold by the monarch as they see fit.

Charles and Anne soon made the best of their new home, running down the long corridors and filling the palace with noisy games and bath times. Charles's games could get loud, but he wasn't allowed to misbehave. When

Charles did misbehave, by sticking his tongue out or putting an ice cube down the back of one of the footmen, he was spanked by either his father or one of his nannies. Unlike today, spanking was a common form of punishment in 1952, even for princes.

The changes weren't just for Charles and Anne. As queen, Elizabeth made changes too. One of these changes was how her children were expected to address her. After her father became king, Elizabeth remembered that instead of calling him Daddy, she and her sister had to call him, "Your Majesty", and curtsey. This made her father sad, and she hadn't liked it much either. Elizabeth didn't want Charles and Anne to have to do the same, so she allowed them to call her Mummy. Elizabeth also changed how people had to address her children. According to tradition, as prince and princess Elizabeth's children should be addressed as His or Her Royal Highness, but Elizabeth insisted they be called Charles and Anne instead.

No Special Treatment

Charles and Anne's lives were very different to those of most children. As well as travelling between palaces, they had chauffeurs, security guards, nannies and hundreds of servants who could get them anything they wanted. Elizabeth and Philip did not want their children to become spoiled. They wanted them to understand how lucky they were and to take good care of their things.

When Charles was five he took one of the dogs out for a walk, but came back without its lead. Charles's parents could have easily bought another one or sent a member of staff to look for it, but they wanted him to learn to look after things. Elizabeth and Philip sent Charles to look for it and told him not come home until he had found it.

Prince Philip didn't want his son to be treated differently, but this wasn't easy. When people saw Charles, they didn't always know how to behave. After a heavy snow, Charles made a pile of snowballs and threw them at a police officer. Had Charles been any other little boy, the officer would have given him a telling off or buried him in so many snowballs he would never try it again; instead the officer said nothing. Prince Philip saw what was happening and told the officer to give Charles as good as he got and pelt him with snowballs right back.

The Prime Minister Can Wait

Elizabeth and Philip didn't want other people to treat their children as if they were special, but that didn't mean they weren't very special to them. Elizabeth had many demands on her time but did her best to rearrange appointments around her children's schedule. One of these appointments was her weekly meeting with the prime minister, which was put back an hour so that she could give Charles and Anne a bath and put them to bed, sometimes wearing her crown!

Elizabeth wore her crown around the palace to get used to its weight. Elizabeth was preparing for a ceremony called a coronation. The crown used in the coronation is called the St Edward's Crown and weighs more than two kilograms.

THE CORONATION

In the United Kingdom, a person officially becomes king or queen at the time of their proclamation, which happens shortly after the death of the previous monarch. The coronation of a new king or queen takes place a number of months after the death of the previous king or queen, to allow time for the funeral as well as a period of mourning. A coronation is a religious ceremony in which a sovereign is crowned and where he or she swears the coronation oath.

In Great Britain, the coronation of a king or queen takes place at Westminster Abbey in London and has done for over 900 years. The ceremony has changed very little during that time. The ceremony is conducted by the archbishop of Canterbury who is the spiritual leader of the Church of England.

In the first part of the ceremony, the archbishop of Canterbury calls on everyone in the abbey to recognize the rightful king or queen before them.

After this, the king or queen promises to serve the United Kingdom by swearing the coronation oath. In the oath, the sovereign swears to govern the peoples of the United Kingdom of Great Britain and Northern Ireland, and the dominions according to their respective laws and customs, and to preserve the Church of England. After swearing the oath, the archbishop performs a traditional Church of England ceremony called a Communion Service.

Then a canopy is held over the sovereign's head while the archbishop anoints him or her with holy oil, dabbing it on the head, hands and chest.

After the anointing, the sovereign is given the Coronation Regalia.

THE CORONATION REGALIA INCLUDES:

The Sovereign's Orb

This golden sphere topped with a jewelled cross is placed in the sovereign's right hand before being returned to the altar. The orb symbolizes the sovereign's role as Head of the Church of England.

The Coronation Ring

The coronation ring is placed on the sovereign's right hand and is a symbol of dignity.

The Sovereign's Sceptre with Cross

The sceptre and cross symbolize the king or queen's power. The Sovereign's Sceptre is topped with the Cullinan I diamond, an enormous 530.2 carat diamond thought to be one of the most valuable in the world.

The Rod of Equity and Mercy

This golden rod is topped with an enamel dove.

The rod symbolizes the king or queen's role in caring for and leading his or her people.

After presenting the regalia, the archbishop of Canterbury places the St Edward's crown on the sovereign's head. The congregation then cries, "Long live the queen!" (or king).

During a coronation ceremony, the heir to the throne is expected to swear an oath to the monarch and lead other people in doing the same. But Charles was too young. The palace decided

Charles could watch the coronation and that he would be taken home if he got too fidgety.

When the day of the coronation came, Charles's nannies dressed him in a white silk suit, and, to make sure he looked extra tidy, the palace barber slicked down his hair with what he described as the "most appalling gunge". While watching the service, Charles tugged at his grandmother's sleeve to ask her lots of questions, but even with her best answers Charles got bored and was taken home.

Charles waited at Buckingham Palace for his parents to return. When they arrived, he joined them out on the balcony to wave to the crowds of people who had come to celebrate his mother, the queen. The parades of men in uniform, the glittering robes, the horses and carriages, it was all for her, and one day it would be for him.

Four-year-old Charles probably didn't spend much time thinking about it, but his parents certainly did. And even though it wasn't likely to happen for a very long time, they wanted to make sure Charles was ready.

AN EDUCATION FIT
FOR A KING

Charles's parents worried that if he wasn't given the right education, he wouldn't be able to handle the pressure that came with being heir to the throne.

Like most children in England, Charles started school in the year he turned five. Instead of travelling to school, Charles's first school came to him. Charles's parents converted one of the rooms in the nursery into a schoolroom, and hired a teacher called a governess to teach him. Her name was Catherine Peebles, or Miss P.

With Miss P, or Mispy, Charles learned his letters and numbers. Charles found reading easy, but he found writing harder. Charles did not like maths. Charles's favourite subject was history. History came easily to Charles because a lot of it was about his own family – the kings and queens of the United Kingdom. Charles was surrounded by history, walking in the footsteps of relatives such as Queen Victoria and Henry VIII. Mispy used some of the palace paintings to help Charles with his studies. As well as exploring the history at home, Mispy replaced Charles's daily walks with his nannies with visits to historic sights and museums around London.

Mispy taught Charles geography, too using a large globe in the school room – something which would soon come in very handy.

Party at the Palace

In November, Charles had not one, but two parties to celebrate his fifth birthday. Charles's first party was on his birthday at Windsor Castle with his grandmother, and the second was an extra-special birthday party at Buckingham Palace. For this party, Charles dressed as Robin Hood with his very own bow and arrow and Anne dressed as a fairy. There was a cake and presents including an

Charles dressed as Robin Hood

electronic dog and a Charles-sized racing car that he could actually drive, with a top speed of eight miles (13 kilometres) per hour.

Goodbye Again

Charles's parents had done everything they could to make Charles's birthday special, because shortly afterwards they set off on a tour of the commonwealth – a tour that kept them away for six months. Queen Elizabeth and Prince Philip kept in touch, but unlike today when people can make calls and send messages wherever they are, Charles's parents had to rely on long-distance telephone calls that could take a long time to connect. They also sent postcards. Charles and Mispy tracked his parents' journey using the globe in the schoolroom, learning about all the different places they stopped along the way.

The Prince Sets Sail

Charles's parents were due to return in the spring of 1954, but rather than wait for them at home, the palace decided it would be more fun for Charles and Anne to meet them along the way. In April, Charles and Anne travelled to Portsmouth to embark an adventure of their very own aboard the brand-new Royal Yacht *Britannia*.

HMY *BRITANNIA*

Her Majesty's Yacht *Britannia* was a 126-metre-long yacht commissioned by King George VI shortly before he died. The royal yacht was designed to allow the royal family to travel in comfort and receive important guests while away from home. In her lifetime, HMY *Britannia* was used for 968 state visits and travelled more than a million nautical miles. *Britannia* was the last of 84 royal yachts built since the 1600s. The royal yacht is no longer used by the royal family, but you can visit *Britannia* in Edinburgh.

It was HMY *Britannia*'s maiden voyage. Charles and Anne had fun exploring the new ship which had a sandpit and a slide to keep them entertained.

When Queen Elizabeth boarded the ship in Tobruk, Libya, the crew lined up to welcome her aboard. After 162 days apart, Charles was excited to see his mother, but he didn't know how he was supposed to greet her. At home he could run to her, but was that the same at sea? Unsure, Charles stood in line, waiting to shake her hand.

Charles and Anne had grown up a lot while their parents were away, and the family used the long voyage back as a chance to share each other's news and get to know each other again.

Queen Elizabeth and Prince Philip with Charles and Anne

Like with any good holiday, Charles came home with souvenirs which included a train set and a saddle from the king of Libya, which would come in useful when he got home.

Charles Takes the Reins

Ever since Charles's mother was a little girl, she had loved horses, playing with toy ones until she was old enough to ride herself. Elizabeth hoped Charles would love horses too. When Charles was six years old, he was given a Welsh pony named William. Charles liked riding, but soon discovered that he wasn't as horse-mad as his mother. Charles was nervous, but with lots of practice he became a good rider. Charles loved other animals too and shared the schoolroom with Harvey the rabbit, Chi-Chi the hamster and a pair of lovebirds named David and Annie.

Charles's teacher, Mispy, liked to keep his lessons interesting and came up with lots of fun ways to help the young prince learn what he needed to. When Charles was seven years old, Mispy began teaching Charles French.

Charles Goes to School

But even with all the historical field trips, animals and French lessons, when Charles was almost eight years old, his parents decided he needed to actually go to school.

Charles was the first heir to the throne to be sent to school. Learning alone with Mispy suited Charles's quiet, sensitive personality, but Philip worried that it wasn't preparing him for public life, where he would have to meet lots of people and learn how to get along with them. Elizabeth hoped sending Charles to school would give him a broader education than the one she had received. Elizabeth and Philip chose a school called Hill House in West London.

On 28 January 1957 Charles dressed in his new uniform and set off for his very first day of school. It was a day unlike anything he had experienced before. Charles painted in the art room, ran around in the school gym and ate his lunch in a room with lots of other chattering boys. When he got home, he told his mother all about it. Elizabeth was pleased that Charles's first day had gone so well. The second day was very different.

Once news had got out that the prince had attended the school, a crowd of press and local people gathered outside to greet him. The mass of people stopped other parents from arriving and made the day very difficult. The headmaster called the palace to tell them what was going on and said that if it continued, Charles would no longer be welcome. The palace called the newspapers and told them to stop. Thankfully they did.

When Charles returned to school, things were much better, but as much as his father hoped he would be treated just like any other pupil, this wasn't always the case. As well as having the picture of his first days at school in all the papers, when Charles's parents came to his Sports Day, his friends and teachers all had to bow.

But some things were ordinary for Charles, since, as well as lessons, pupils at Hill House were expected help maintain the school. Charles's jobs were to sweep the floor and wash up after lunch. Charles also learned to ride the bus, and how to use money to pay his fare, though he was the only passenger whose mother's face was on the coins!

Like other pupils, Charles caught coughs, colds and tonsillitis, and often had to miss school. Charles's tonsils caused him to miss so much school that he had an operation to have them removed. After the operation, Charles asked to keep his tonsils in a little jar, which he took with him wherever he went for months afterwards.

Moving On

When Charles returned to school after his surgery, it wasn't long before he had to leave again. Pupils stayed at Hill House until they were around nine years old. Elizabeth and Philip needed to decide where they wanted to send him next. Prince Philip believed they should look no further than the school he attended when he was Charles's age, a school named Cheam School in Hampshire.

Cheam School would mean big changes for Charles. Hill House was a day school, which meant

Charles went home to Buckingham Palace at the end of each day and spent his weekends at home with his family. Cheam School was almost 100 kilometres from Buckingham Palace and was a boarding school. This meant that instead of coming home at the end of the day, pupils stayed at the school overnight and even at weekends. Charles started at Cheam School in September 1957.

LEAVING HOME

Life at Cheam School was about as different from Buckingham Palace as it could get and Charles found it very difficult. Instead of his own warm, comfortable room in his nursery, at Cheam School, Charles slept in a hard bed in a cold dormitory with seven other boys. Charles missed his home, his family and his nannies very much, and at night he hugged his teddy bear and cried.

If Charles was sad at night, the days weren't that much better. An alarm sounded at 7.15 every morning, when he had to wash and dress himself and go down for breakfast. Breakfast was eaten at long tables and boys were expected to take turns serving the food. Lessons started at 9.00 am and went on until 1.00 pm with a short break for a snack. At the end of the day, instead of getting to go home, Charles had to go back to the cold dormitory with the other boys.

No Friends for Charles

Charles's parents sent him to school so that he would be treated like any other boy, but this didn't happen. Even though Charles slept in a dormitory with other boys and wore the same uniform, there was no getting away from the fact that one day he would be king.

Some children didn't want to be friends with Charles because they didn't want to be seen to suck up to him. Others assumed that because Charles was a prince it meant he thought he was better than them. Some children were mean and teased him for having big ears and called him fatty.

In the afternoons, students at Cheam were expected to take part in sports. Philip had loved sport at school and was good at it, but Charles, no matter how hard he tried, was not. During the holidays, Prince Philip practised with Charles whenever he got the chance, but nothing seemed to help. Charles did his best to fit in, even breaking school rules for which he received beatings from the headmaster.

Methods of 'corporal punishment' such as beating or caning were common forms of discipline in UK schools in the 1950s. Corporal punishment was made illegal in state schools in England and Wales in 1986, and private schools, like the one Charles attended, in 1998.

As well as being homesick, Charles was often physically sick too, catching colds, flu, measles and even appendicitis, spending time in the school sick room with the nurse.

The Prying Press

When Charles went to Cheam, his parents hoped actually staying at the school would keep him away from reporters but it didn't stop them. Even though they had been asked to leave the prince alone, some reporters called the school and even visited to ask about him. When they did not receive answers, some reporters chose to make up stories or even paid other students to share what they knew.

One story stated that Charles didn't get much pocket money from his parents. A source claimed that Charles sold his possessions to other students to buy sweets in the school tuck shop. Despite being untrue, the story appeared in papers across the world. Reading of the prince's plight and eager to help, the Retail Candy Stores Institute of America organized a delivery of forty-eight large tins of sweets to the school – a gift the prince could not accept.

A Message from Mummy

In the summer of 1958, Charles was invited to the headmaster's office with some school friends to watch the opening of the Commonwealth Games (then called the Empire and Commonwealth Games) held in Cardiff Arms Park, Wales. The queen was not able to attend the closing ceremony, but she did record a message that was played to the crowd and the viewers watching at home and at school. In her message, the queen said she wanted to use this exciting event in Wales to announce that she was creating her "son Charles, Prince of Wales, today" and that she would formalize his appointment at a ceremony when he was older. The crowd in the stadium cheered and cries of "God Bless the Prince of Wales" rang around the stadium. In the headmaster's study, Charles's friends congratulated him and patted him on the back, but instead of feeling proud or excited, Charles was embarrassed to be the centre of attention and he blushed to the tips of his ears.

THE PRINCES OF WALES

The area of the United Kingdom we know as Wales was once made up of three powerful principalities, Deheubarth, Powys and Gwynedd. Each of these principalities had its own prince and all were independent of England.

In 1258, one of these princes, Llywelyn ap Gruffudd, proclaimed himself the king, or prince, of all three principalities and became the first Prince of Wales. His title, Prince of Wales, was recognized in a treaty with King Henry III of England, in return for Llywelyn's allegiance. But after Henry's death, Llywelyn refused to pledge his allegiance to his son King Edward I. King Edward I wanted to conquer Wales, Scotland and Ireland and unite them under his kingship. In 1282, King Edward I of England led troops into Wales to conquer the territory for the English Crown. Prince Llywelyn was offered many deals in order to hand over the crown, including a title and a vast amount of land, but Prince Llywelyn refused. Prince Llywelyn ap Gruffudd and his troops fought bravely but he was killed on 11 December 1282. After his death, King Edward ordered that Prince Llywelyn's head be cut off and paraded through the streets of London and mocked as king of the outlaws. Llywelyn's head was displayed on a spike outside the Tower of London for more than fifteen years. After his death, Llywelyn's brother Dafydd became Prince of Wales and took control of the Welsh fighters. Prince Dafydd was captured in October 1283 and hanged, drawn and quartered by order of the king. His head was mounted on a spike like his brother.

After his conquest, King Edward I divided the land between himself and his supporters. He also seized many Welsh historic treasures. Edward I built stone castles to prevent the Welsh people from rising up and defeating him.

In 1284, Edward I had a son, born in Caernarfon Castle. Legend has it that Edward I promised the Welsh people that he would give them their own prince to rule over them. A prince who spoke no word of English, but this was a trick. Edward declared his infant son, who was too young to speak any language, Prince of Wales. Since then, it has been a tradition of the monarch of the United Kingdom to give the title Prince of Wales to their heir.

Influencer in Training

....

While other students didn't want to hang out with Charles, they did want to be like him. When Charles got a new pencil case, other pupils wrote home to ask for one just like his. Although Charles didn't like being centre of attention, he didn't mind being centre stage in drama class. In fact, Charles discovered he loved to act and was good at it, earning a rave review from the school paper for his portrayal of one of his royal predecessors, King Richard III.

Charles liked working with the other actors and pulling together as a team. On stage he could pretend to be anyone, so it didn't matter that he was a prince. But if Charles thought he could get away with being just another member of the cast when the show ended, he was mistaken. After the curtains closed on 19 February 1960, the headmaster stepped on to the stage to announce to the audience that the queen had given birth to a boy, Charles's younger brother, Prince Andrew.

Charles spent five years at Cheam School and despite not being exceptional in the classroom or on the playing field, he was made head boy in his final year. Charles's teachers commented that the young prince was kind and sensitive and had good manners.

Like Father, Unlike Son

When he wasn't at school or unwell, Charles loved spending time outdoors, hunting with his father at Sandringham and Balmoral or fishing with his great-uncle, Lord Mountbatten. Charles enjoyed his time away from school, but things at home were not easy for him either. Philip was disappointed that his son didn't enjoy school. Philip believed school had given him confidence, but it did not have the same effect on Charles, who seemed even more shy than before.

Charles found comfort in the company of his grandmother and his nanny Mabel Anderson.

After seeing how miserable her grandson had been at Cheam, the Queen Mother begged Elizabeth and Philip to send Charles somewhere closer. She thought Eton would be a good choice as it was close to Windsor Castle. Philip and

Elizabeth worried that Eton was also too close to London and the newspapers. Philip decided another of his old schools was just the place: Gordonstoun, Scotland.

On 1 April 1962, Philip made sure Charles arrived for his first day in style, flying him to RAF Lossiemouth himself and then driving him the last half mile. Philip was excited for Charles. His time at Gordonstoun had been some of the best years of his life and he hoped Charles would enjoy it as much as he did.

Low Times in the Highlands

But Charles was very different to his father. Charles found it hard to make friends at the best of times, but what happened when he arrived at Gordonstoun made it almost impossible. Bullying was common at the school, and younger pupils were often beaten up by older ones or trapped in baskets and placed under the cold showers. This treatment was considered a rite of passage at the school. Though it was harsh and painful, once students had experienced it, they were considered part of the gang. When Charles entered the school, the housemaster told the boys that if he heard that Prince Charles had been bullied in any way, the person responsible would be expelled. To make sure nobody got into trouble, Charles's classmates got together and agreed to ignore the prince completely. Any student who was seen to make friends with Charles was punished by the others. This made life very lonely for Charles.

One place Charles wasn't ignored was on the rugby pitch. There he was a target for his classmates, who took the opportunity to tackle, punch and stamp on him whenever they could.

Charles's nights were just as bad. Charles's dormitory, which he shared with fourteen other boys, was a hut with hard wooden beds. The hut was so old – all of the windows were kept open and let in the cold wind. Charles's bunkmates weren't any warmer; now out of the sight of the housemaster, they tormented Charles while he was trying to sleep.

In a letter home, Charles wrote, "It's such hell here especially at night. I don't get any sleep practically at all nowadays ... The people in my dormitory are foul. Goodness they are horrid. I don't know how anyone could be so foul. They throw slippers all night long or hit me with pillows."

School Life

Gordonstoun taught the usual subjects such as English, Latin (which was common in schools at the time), and maths. Charles was well behaved, but he wasn't exceptional in any particular subject. Charles enjoyed art, drawing and painting and learning pottery. In the afternoons the students did sports such as hockey (Charles's favourite), and cricket (Charles's least favourite), as well as rugby. Charles was an excellent swimmer and earned his life-saving certificate to become a member of the school's surf rescue team. Gordonstoun also offered outdoor activities such as canoeing and sailing.

The Cherry Brandy Incident

Sailing gave the boys the chance to explore. One afternoon, Charles and his schoolmates sailed to Stornoway Harbour and went into a local hotel. The other boys had done this before without causing a stir, but it was different with Charles in tow. Hearing that the young prince was in town, people headed to the hotel to catch a glimpse of him. Then a reporter arrived and started taking pictures. Charles was embarrassed and wanted to get away. He left his friends and walked into the next room of the hotel, which was the bar. Unsure of what to do, but not wanting to just stand there, Charles ordered a cherry brandy.

Later, Charles said he did what he thought would draw the least attention. But Charles wasn't any other customer, he was a prince, and he was only fourteen. As Charles sat down with his drink, a journalist walked in.

Charles's security officer whisked him away into a car and back to school, but it was too late. News of what became known as "the Cherry Brandy Incident" filled the papers for days. But the story didn't just embarrass the prince. The incident damaged the reputation of the school, as people questioned how such a thing could be allowed to happen. It damaged the reputation of his parents who were criticized for raising a wayward son and it lost his security officer, a man Charles respected, his job. Charles was devastated.

Royal Writings

This wasn't the only story that made the papers. If one of your school books went missing you probably wouldn't think much of it. But when Prince Charles's exercise book went missing, it ended up in the hands of the newspapers. The British papers refused to print the essays and returned it to the school, but not before someone sent copies to newspapers abroad. The essays were published in a German newspaper three days after Charles's sixteenth birthday. They were later published in the USA. There was nothing scandalous in the essays. They were about subjects such as television, and what he would take with him to a desert island.

To make up for the fact the essays weren't all that exciting, the newspaper claimed that the prince had sold them. Once again Charles was embarrassed and alone.

When Charles was not at school, he complained about it to anyone who would listen. Charles's mother didn't understand. She had never been to school. She had been taught at home and was kept out of the view of the press until she was much older than Charles. Prince Philip couldn't understand him either. He wanted Charles to use the challenges he faced at school to build his confidence and self-esteem.

But Charles was very different from his father and his situation was different, too. Charles was very different from everyone. Nobody, not even people in his own family, had been through anything like what he was going through. At a time in his life when most people want to hide and fit in, Charles was on the front page. He couldn't even escape when he went skiing.

Charles had wanted to try skiing for a long time, but his first holiday was ruined by photographers who followed him on the slopes trying to get pictures of him when he was making his first slips. Charles found it hard to concentrate with such a crowd around him. The palace had to make a deal with the papers, allowing them to take pictures of Charles in the afternoons if they left him alone in the mornings. With time to learn away from the cameras, Charles became a good skier.

A Taste of Working Life

In 1965, Charles got a taste of what his life would be like when school was over and he became a working royal, accompanying his parents on official visits. The first of these was in January when he attended the funeral of former Prime Minister Sir Winston Churchill with his parents. In June he attended a garden party at the Palace of Holyroodhouse in Edinburgh. Charles was usually shy when he talked to new people, but he did well at the party, stopping to talk to the other guests for longer than he needed to.

Back at school, Charles did his best to get along with people and studied hard. Charles enjoyed music. He took lessons in the trumpet and the cello and sang in the choir. He also performed in school plays, taking on the role of Macbeth, once again getting rave reviews. Charles felt more confident when he could pretend to be someone else.

Palace of Holyroodhouse

Examining Royalty

At the end of the year, Charles took his O-levels – exams similar to today's GCSEs. Charles was the first heir to the throne ever to sit public exams, which meant that this would be the first time ordinary people could compare their achievements with a member of the royal family.

Charles achieved six O-levels. The teachers at Gordonstoun were pleased with his progress but Charles still wasn't happy there.

At the end of term, Charles left, excited to travel up to Balmoral and fish with his father. He was also excited because after the holiday he wasn't returning to Gordonstoun – instead he was going to Australia.

GROWING UP

Charles's trip to Australia wasn't a Royal Tour. His parents thought he was too young for that and far too shy. Instead they arranged for Charles to study at a school in Australia and board with other students, just as he did at Gordonstoun. His parents hoped it would help Charles get to know Australia and what Australians were like, and also give Australians a chance to know him, as one day he would be their king.

On 3 February 1966, Charles arrived at the Timbertop Campus of the Geelong Church of England Grammar School. The Australian press wanted to know everything about the prince and what he would be doing. To give them what they needed, photographers and journalists were invited to accompany Charles on his first day at the school but were then expected to leave him alone for the rest of his stay.

The curriculum at Timbertop was different

to Gordonstoun. There was very little sitting in classrooms. Instead, students spent most of their time outdoors, learning to fend for themselves. Students had to chop wood for the boilers, work the land to grow food for the school and look after the farm animals. Students could hike, run and fish. Though the rivers were very different to the ones at Balmoral, Charles used his fishing experience to help teach the younger boys at the school.

It was hard work. Charles fed the pigs, cleaned out disgusting fly traps and his hands were blistered from chopping wood. But Charles felt like he fitted in and made friends. Away from Gordonstoun and the press, Charles felt his confidence growing. He was free to try things and fail, without being watched. He was free to succeed, too.

While at Timbertop, Charles had to study for his A-levels. Unlike Gordonstoun where there were teachers watching over his work Charles had to manage his studying himself and found he enjoyed working independently.

During his second term at the school, the weather turned cold. It snowed and Charles taught some of the younger students to ski.

By the time Charles left Australia he felt like it had become a second home and he couldn't wait for his chance to return.

A Happy Prince

On the flight home, Charles's plane stopped at Brisbane, Australia. Crowds of people had gathered at the airport to see him. A member of Charles's staff told him that he should greet them. Charles was nervous. He'd not done something like this by himself before, but when he approached the people, he saw they were smiling. Charles smiled too. Later, Charles said he felt something change inside him, and that from that moment on he didn't feel uncomfortable meeting people anymore.

Back at Gordonstoun, it was Charles's final year at the school. He was more confident and the teachers decided that he should be Head Boy, just as his father had been thirty years before him. In 1967, like thousands of young people around the country, Charles sat his A-levels. Charles was nervous. Not because his future depended upon his results – Charles's future had been decided the moment he was born. Charles was nervous because his results would be printed in the newspapers. Charles took History and French and achieved a B and a C. Charles told his parents that he would like to continue his studies at university.

Charles Goes to University

To decide which university Charles should go to, the palace called a meeting. The meeting included the queen's private secretary, the prime minister and the archbishop of Canterbury. It did not include Charles. After several hours they decided that Charles should go to Trinity

College, Cambridge, and then to Dartmouth Naval College before joining the Royal Navy.

Charles was not the first heir to the throne to attend university. Both his great-great-grandfather and his great-uncle had studied at university, although neither completed a degree. Edward VII lived away from the college and expected lecturers to travel to him. Edward VIII lived in college and spent most of his time socializing and holding drunken dinner parties. Charles wanted to live with other students and earn a degree. He chose to study archaeology and anthropology but later changed to history.

Charles found he fit in well at Cambridge. Despite the fact Trinity attracted students from a variety of backgrounds, he made friends with people with whom he had the most in common. People whose parents owned big houses and were interested in hunting and playing polo.

THE POLO-PLAYING PRINCE

Charles was a keen polo player and played on the college team. He grew up watching his father, Prince Philip, play polo at Windsor, just as his mother had watched her father King George VI play when she was young. Lord Mountbatten taught Prince Philip to play, and when Charles could ride well enough, Prince Philip passed on what he had learned to his son.

Polo is a ball game played by two teams of four players riding specially trained horses. Players have long mallets which they swing to try to hit a wooden ball down the polo field between the opposing team's goal. To make sure the horses have enough speed to play, polo players need as many as eight animals in order to be able to switch mounts multiple times during a game. Polo is one of the most expensive sports in the world. Players need to be experienced riders in order to be able to take part.

No Parties for the Prince

As well as sports, university is also a place where many students become interested in politics and join clubs and societies relating to the causes that most appeal to them. While Charles was at university, he asked his advisor, Lord Richard Butler, if it would be appropriate for him to join one of these groups. Lord Butler was the head of Trinity College and a former cabinet minister. Lord Butler told Charles that although he might have lots of opinions, unlike other students he was not free to express them by joining political societies. As a future monarch it was important for Charles not to appear to favour any particular side.

POLITICALLY NEUTRAL

While it is not technically against the law, it is considered unconstitutional for the king or queen to vote in elections in the United Kingdom because they have to appear to be politically neutral. As monarch, the king or queen will have to work with whoever is elected into office and therefore it is important that they have not spoken or voted for or against either side. Other members of the royal family are also expected to keep their political views to themselves and support the monarch by not voting.

The Performing Prince

One society Prince Charles was allowed to join was a drama society. Prince Charles had enjoyed taking part in plays at school and was keen to get involved in university too. Charles joined a society named The Cambridge Footlights. The Cambridge Footlights was famous for being the place where many of the United Kingdom's most famous actors and comedians started their careers. Prince Charles became a popular performer with the Footlights, performing in comedy sketches and doing impressions of famous people from history and around the college, including a singing dustman who made the news after Charles complained about his singing waking him up in the morning.

As well as Prince Charles, famous former members of Cambridge Footlights include Emma Thompson, Stephen Fry, Richard Ayoade and Simon Bird.

Charles had more freedom than he had done at school and he had his own rooms to retreat to. He found it easier to make friends, too. Charles did well at his studies and scored above average in his first exams.

But while Charles had been able to choose his subjects, and the societies he joined, unlike most of the other students he was unable to choose what he wanted to do when he left. As heir to the throne, it was his duty to take his place as a working member of the royal family. A duty that was coming closer by the day.

DUTY CALLS

In 1969, Charles's studies at Cambridge were interrupted. When Charles was nine years old, his mother had named him Prince of Wales – a title traditionally given by the monarch to the heir to throne. When Queen Elizabeth made the announcement, she promised that this title would be formalized in a ceremony when Charles was older. Ten years on, the time had come for the ceremony, called an investiture, to take place at Caernarfon Castle, Wales.

Growing up, Charles had spent very little time in Wales. The palace felt it would be appropriate for Charles to take some time away from Cambridge to study Welsh language and history. Charles was not happy about this. He was happy at Cambridge and didn't want to leave, but Charles's future was not his own.

Protesting a Prince

Many people in Wales weren't happy about it either. So many in fact, a popular song in Wales at the time was a song titled "Carlo". The song, sung in Welsh, made fun of a polo-playing prince called Carlo Windsor, who lived in Buckingham Palace. People felt that the British government was sending Charles to increase Welsh support for him as prince, and to decrease the support for the Welsh Nationalists, who were fighting for Welsh independence and who didn't believe Wales should have an English prince.

To protest the arrival of the prince, Welsh nationalists organized demonstrations and staged hunger strikes to draw attention to their cause.

THE FIGHT FOR WELSH INDEPENDENCE

The Welsh Nationalists and the Welsh Nationalist Party, *Plaid Cymru*, had nothing personal against Charles. Instead, they did not like what Charles represented – rule by the British crown and the British government. The Welsh Nationalists believed that British rule had led people to forget about the unique culture, language and history of Wales. They felt that the British government exploited Welsh resources, such as coal and farmland, and ignored the needs of Welsh people. Support for the nationalists grew in the 1960s following events such as the flooding of Capel Celyn and the Aberfan disaster.

The Flooding of Capel Celyn

In 1965, the British government approved an application to flood the Tryweryn Valley, home to Capel Celyn – one of the last Welsh-only speaking villages in Wales. The application was from Liverpool City Council who wanted to build a reservoir to provide water for the growing English city. Despite fierce Welsh protest, around 70 people living in Capel Celyn were forced to leave their homes and watch as their rural community was destroyed.

The Disaster at Aberfan

In October 1966, 144 people in the Welsh village of Aberfan were killed when a coal mine's waste heap collapsed. The heap, which towered over the village, was poorly maintained by the owners of the mine. The disaster buried homes in the village as well as Pantglas Junior School, killing 116 children. After the disaster, people in Wales were angry with the lack of support from the British government. Many in Wales believed the government would have acted differently if the disaster had taken place in an English village and to an English school.

Despite the protests, Charles travelled to Aberystwyth to study Welsh history and language in April 1969. Life at university wasn't easy for

Charles. Students at the university staged protests most days and made a pact to speak to Charles only in Welsh. This left Charles feeling alone.

Charles's teacher, a man named Dr Tedi Millward, explained why. Dr Millward was vice president of the Welsh Nationalist Party, *Plaid Cymru*. As well as Welsh language, Dr Millward taught Charles about Welsh Nationalism and why many people in Wales did not welcome him. He also taught him how hundreds of years of British rule had led to the decline of Welsh culture and language and that people believed they had to fight to preserve it.

Despite their differences, Prince Charles and Dr Millward got on well. Charles learned Welsh and Dr Millward helped him use it to write a speech to read at the investiture.

Tensions Rise

As the day of the investiture approached, tensions rose in the town of Caernarfon. Strict nationalist groups threatened to attack the ceremony and some laid bombs around the town. Two devices exploded, one killing the men setting it. People feared for the security of the event. Extra police from around the country were brought in to make sure things went according to plan.

On 1 July 1969, Charles was also nervous about security. As he and his family rode through the streets towards the castle, Charles watched the crowd closely and was relieved when nobody threw anything at them.

A Historic Occasion

In the ruined remains of Caernarfon Castle, Charles knelt before his mother as she presented him with the symbols of office as Prince of Wales.

Charles's investiture as Prince of Wales

These symbols included a silver sword, a golden rod symbolizing justice and government, an amethyst ring symbolizing unity with Wales, a purple silk cloak and a golden crown.

Charles then pledged himself to his mother, the queen, and to the people of Wales.

After this, it was time for Charles to make a speech in Welsh to the people of Wales, and to the millions around the world watching on television. For a moment, Charles panicked that he had lost it, only to discover he had sat on it.

With speech in hand, Charles thanked the people of Wales for what they had taught him during his stay and promised to serve them faithfully.

"YN WIR, RWY'N BWRIADU CYSYLLTU FY HUN O DDIFRIF MEWN GAIR A GWEITHRED A CHYMAINT

O FYWYD Y DYWYSOGAETH - A'R FATH DYWYSOGAETH YDY HI! — AG A FYDD YN BOSIBL."

"IT IS, INDEED, MY FIRM INTENTION TO ASSOCIATE MYSELF IN WORD AND DEED WITH AS MUCH OF THE LIFE OF THE PRINCIPALITY AS POSSIBLE — AND WHAT A PRINCIPALITY!"

Charles, Prince of Wales

Prince Popular

While there were some who protested Charles's ceremony, others showed their support, holding street parties celebrating the new prince. Children in Wales were given the day off school, and the ceremony was watched by millions of people all over the world. The dramatic ceremony put a spotlight on Wales and Welsh culture. After the ceremony, Charles went on a week-long tour of Wales where he was met by cheering crowds of people wishing him well.

A Final Blow

On the final day of the tour, Charles was in Cardiff when another bomb exploded and severely injured an eleven-year-old boy. Charles wanted to go and visit the boy but was told that such a visit might excite him too much. Instead, Charles wrote to him and donated towards his rehabilitation.

Despite this and the protests, the palace felt Charles's investiture and his time in Wales had been a success, both for the monarchy and for Wales.

Charles returned to Cambridge in October to study for his final exams. The ceremony and the tour were over, but for Charles, his life as a working member of the royal family was only just beginning.

Prince Charles held his twenty-first birthday at Buckingham Palace and invited over 400 guests. There were fireworks in the palace gardens, an orchestra and a rock band, which played to guests who danced until dawn.

The Prince Means Business

During the Easter Holidays, Charles paused his studies again to fly to Australia to take part in events commemorating 200 years since the arrival of Captain Cook in 1770.

On the way home, the palace scheduled a stop in Japan to visit Tokyo. But Charles wasn't there as a tourist. This was part of his work as a royal. One of the reasons the government sends members of the royal family abroad is for them to represent the British people to promote Great Britain as a place to do business. In Tokyo, Charles dined with the emperor and met with the heads of major Japanese corporations. Meetings like these are important as they can help build trade relationships for United Kingdom and create jobs for the people living there. For many people, it is an honour to meet with a member of the royal family. Business leaders met with the prince and showed him what they were working on.

During his trip, Charles met with the president of the Sony corporation who mentioned that he was planning to build a new factory in Europe. When Charles, as representative of Wales, urged the president to consider building his factory there, the president of Sony agreed. Four years later the factory opened in Glamorgan, providing jobs for the people living there for many years.

A Royal Degree

Charles's duties had taken him away more than he would have liked. He still had to sit his exams. In summer 1970, Prince Charles was awarded a lower second-class degree. Like all the graduating students, Charles learned a lot at

Cambridge, but unlike most of them, his results wouldn't affect which jobs he could apply for. Plans for Charles's future had been made a long time ago and it was time for them to take flight.

Charles's father, Prince Philip, and both his great-grandfathers had served in the Royal Navy, and in 1970, the palace announced that Charles would do the same after spending some time with the Royal Air Force, training as a jet pilot.

A Flight of Fancy

Before Charles took on his new role, he had time for some fun with his friends. In his spare time, Charles enjoyed hunting, fishing and playing polo (see page 104). It was at a polo match at Windsor in 1970 that twenty-two-year-old Charles met a woman named Camilla Shand. Charles and Camilla had a lot in common. They loved the outdoors and had a similar sense of humour. Charles liked Camilla immediately. He thought she was beautiful, and very funny, and the two became a couple.

In March 1971, Charles began his jet pilot training at the Royal Air Force College at Cranwell.

"I AM ENTERING THE RAF AND THE NAVY BECAUSE I BELIEVE I CAN CONTRIBUTE SOMETHING TO THIS COUNTRY BY SO DOING. TO ME IT IS A WORTHWHILE OCCUPATION AND ONE I AM CONVINCED WILL STAND ME IN GOOD STEAD FOR THE REST OF MY LIFE."

Charles, Prince of Wales

If Charles thought his studying days were over, he got a rude awakening when he arrived at Cranwell. As well as training in flying, Charles had to learn about all the different parts of the aircraft and how the instruments worked. He also had to tackle an old enemy. Charles had hated maths at school, but to complete the course Charles had to pass tests in arithmetic, geometry and algebra.

Charles found the training difficult, but knew if he did not pass, he would not qualify as a pilot. The jets he was training to fly were not only deadly weapons; they were also worth hundreds of thousands of pounds. Even though Charles was the son of the queen, the head of the armed forces, he still needed to prove he was safe to fly. After five months, Charles passed and proved to his commanding officers that he was ready to fly a jet capable of flying 500 miles (805 kilometres) per hour, all by himself.

Head over Heels

In July 1971, Charles took a great leap when he

made his first parachute jump over Studland Bay, Dorset. In the aircraft, Charles was nervous, but he was excited to find out what it was like. Charles exited the plane as planned, but when his parachute opened, he found he was falling upside down. The prince's legs were caught up in the lines to the canopy. Charles had no choice but to untangle himself as quickly as he could. It was a dangerous situation, but the prince landed safely, exhilarated and proud of his presence of mind.

Charles's parachute jump

Charles spent five months with the RAF. Charles liked wearing his uniform because he looked like any other serviceman. It was the first time in his life he felt as though he blended in.

All at Sea

After the RAF, Charles turned his attention to the navy, studying at Britannia Royal Naval College, Dartmouth. At Dartmouth he took a six-week course where he learned about the structure of the Royal Navy, its customs and the art of leadership. When away from his studies, Charles learned to surf and joined the college SCUBA diving club.

The courses were tough, and the skills of being a seaman didn't come naturally to Charles. He had to work hard, but he succeeded and on 5 November 1971 Charles took his place as sub-lieutenant aboard his first ship, the HMS *Norfolk* stationed in the Mediterranean.

Onboard, Charles worried that he was not only out at sea, but that he was also out of his depth. Charles found navigating impossible and even getting around the ship was difficult.

After finding his feet, or sea legs, on HMS *Norfolk*, in 1972 Charles was transferred to HMS *Minerva*. While Charles was in the Mediterranean it was easy for him to come home on leave. When Charles had time off from the navy, he took up royal duties attending functions as well as spending time with his girlfriend, Camilla.

Long Distance

In February 1973, HMS *Minerva* was posted to the Caribbean. Travelling with the navy made Camilla and Charles's relationship difficult. They kept in touch writing letters, but eventually broke up. Camilla wrote to Charles to tell him she was marrying someone else. Charles was heartbroken.

In November 1973, Charles travelled home to attend his sister Anne's wedding to Captain Mark Philips at Westminster Abbey. Watching the royal wedding of Charles's younger sister, many wondered when the prince would settle down. But Charles had other things on his mind: his career at sea and what he was going to do when it was over.

Thinking of the Future

Throughout Charles's time in the navy, he thought about what he was going to do when he left. The title 'Prince of Wales' didn't come with any power, but Charles believed that it did come with influence and he wanted to use that influence to help people.

"I DON'T WANT TO BE A FIGUREHEAD. I WANT TO HELP GET THINGS DONE."

Charles, Prince of Wales

In 1972, Charles watched a programme on television about the challenges faced by young people growing up in disadvantaged communities. Communities with poverty and unemployment, and where opportunities were few and far between. Charles wanted to know if there was something he could do to help. Charles spoke to his advisors and began contacting people working with these communities to find out more.

Charles continued this conversation throughout his time in the navy. Charles's idea was to set up an organization to help young people achieve their ambitions. This help would be in the form of grant money that could be put towards equipment, training or whatever the young person needed to take the next step towards their goal.

A Prince with a Plan

Charles raised the idea with the palace staff and with members of the government, but most people he spoke to told him that the idea was too risky and that if it failed it would damage his reputation. Charles was determined. In 1974, Charles decided that he would begin with an experimental programme to see how it would work. Charles was encouraged by the results and on 25 June 1975, Charles made a speech to the House of Lords announcing his plans to set up a scheme for disadvantaged youth. This would become the Prince's Trust (see page 181).

Aye, Aye, Captain!

Charles took up the post of captain on HMS *Bronington* – a small coastal mine hunter. At twenty-seven years old, Charles was young to be a captain, but he had learned a lot since falling down hatches on HMS *Norfolk*. His training and service on a variety of ships had given him what he needed. But *Bronington* presented a new challenge – seasickness.

While serving as captain, Charles was given orders to follow a Russian submarine detected off the east coast of the United Kingdom. Charles and his crew were given the task of following the submarine and making sure it left British waters without doing any harm.

Charles said goodbye to the navy and HMS *Bronington* in 1976. Charles had enjoyed his time in the navy and had been well-loved by his crew. To show that Charles fit in with the rest of the crew, when he left the ship for the last time, the crew pushed him to shore in a wheelchair with a toilet seat inscribed with the words HMS *Bronington* hung around his neck.

Charles spent a total of five years in the Royal Navy and learned a lot, but it was never his or the palace's intention that he should make the navy his career. Charles did not know when he would be king, but he knew it wasn't likely to happen for a long time. Charles wanted to make the most of his years as heir.

IN SEARCH OF A PRINCESS

The plan, agreed on by the palace when Charles left Gordonstoun, was complete. Charles had his degree from Cambridge, had been invested as Prince of Wales and served his time in the armed forces. As a full-time working royal, Charles's life would now be filled with attending events, receiving foreign guests and working with charities. But Charles had another even more important duty to attend to: finding a bride.

Charles was twenty-eight years old and was considered one of the most eligible bachelors in the world. The woman who married Charles would become very famous. She would become a princess and when Charles became king, queen consort. If she had children, her first-born son would one day be king. It was important that Charles choose not only someone he loved, but someone who was able to deal with the pressure of being in the royal family, of being watched and judged by the press and living a life that was often not her own. Charles was in no hurry to decide.

"YOU HAVE GOT TO CHOOSE SOMEBODY VERY CAREFULLY WHO COULD FULFIL THIS PARTICULAR ROLE, BECAUSE PEOPLE ... WOULD EXPECT QUITE A LOT FROM SOMEBODY LIKE THAT AND IT HAS GOT TO BE SOMEBODY PRETTY SPECIAL."

Charles, Prince of Wales, 1969

While the prince was in no rush, the newspapers were, regularly running stories about who his future bride might be.

In 1977, Charles dated a woman named Sarah Spencer, who lived in a grand house in Northamptonshire called Althorp House. Charles was visiting Sarah at her house for a party when he met her sister, Diana, in a field. Diana was only sixteen and Charles remembered thinking that she was "jolly". Later, Diana recalled that she had thought he was "pretty amazing". Charles and Sarah stopped seeing each other when Sarah revealed in a magazine interview that she was not in love with him.

Following this, Charles dated a woman named Amanda Knatchbull. Amanda was the granddaughter of Charles's great-uncle, Lord Louis Mountbatten. Amanda was a good friend of Charles's family, and the pair had a lot in common. Charles loved Amanda, but when Charles proposed, Amanda turned him down. Amanda told Charles that while she cared for him deeply, she did not think she was suited to public life.

Sudden Sorrow

On 27 August 1979, Charles's world was rocked by the assassination of his great-uncle, Lord Louis Mountbatten, on a boat off the west coast of Ireland. Terrorists had planted an explosive device on the boat which detonated offshore, killing not only Mountbatten but also his grandson and a member of the crew. An organization known as the IRA claimed responsibility for the attack.

WHAT IS THE IRA?

Before 1921, all of the land that we now know as Northern Ireland and the Republic of Ireland had been ruled by the British for hundreds of years.

Many people living in Ireland believed that the British government, acting on behalf of the British crown, exploited the Irish people and that British troops treated them cruelly, forcing them off their land and leaving them to starve. There were many acts of war and rebellion over the centuries and in 1919 the Irish Republican Army (IRA) was formed to fight for an independent Ireland.

In 1921, following a war known as the Irish War of Independence, British and Irish leaders signed a treaty which granted twenty-six southern counties of Ireland independence from British rule. These twenty-six counties became the Republic of Ireland. Most of the people living in the Republic of Ireland were Catholic, a branch of the Christian faith which is led by the Pope in Rome.

Six counties in the north of Ireland were to remain a part of the United Kingdom and become known as Northern Ireland. Many people living Northern Ireland wanted to remain part of the United Kingdom. These people were called Unionists. Unionists were mostly Protestants.

People living in Northern Ireland who did not wish to remain part of the United Kingdom were called Nationalists. Most Nationalists were Catholic. Some of these Nationalists formed the IRA. The IRA believed that attacking targets in Northern Ireland and in mainland Britain would bring an end to British rule. These terror attacks included shooting and bombing civilian and military targets and attacking people with power and influence such as the prime minister and members of the royal family such as Lord Louis Mountbatten.

After much conflict and years of negotiations, in 1998, the British and Irish governments signed an agreement called the Good Friday Agreement (also known as the Belfast

Agreement). The Good Friday Agreement granted Northern Ireland its own government called the Northern Ireland Assembly, made up of Nationalists and Unionists working together. While the Good Friday Agreement did a lot to bring peace to Northern Ireland, the tensions between Unionists and Nationalists in Northern Ireland continue to this day.

Charles was devastated by the loss of his great-uncle. Lord Mountbatten had been a mentor to Charles, writing to him when he was at school, and inviting him to stay during the holidays. Lord Mountbatten had listened to Charles in a way his father had not, and had played a big part in helping make the plan that saw Charles go to Cambridge and into the navy.

As well as feeling sad at the loss, Charles also saw how fiercely groups such as the IRA disliked his family, and what it represented, and that the security he had grown up surrounded by was there for a reason.

A Place to Call Home

After travelling the world with the navy, and moving between royal palaces and boarding school, Charles wanted a place he could call his own. A place that hadn't been designed and decorated by ancestors, but which reflected who he was.

In 1980, Charles bought a house in Gloucestershire called Highgrove House. The house had nine bedrooms and an enormous garden. Both the inside and the outside of the house needed a lot of work, but Charles was most interested in the garden, and set to work designing the grounds with a cottage garden, a meadow of wildflowers and an arboretum.

Love in Loss

Charles was still reeling from losing his great-uncle when he met a familiar face at a friend's house. It was Diana, his ex-girlfriend Sarah Spencer's younger sister. Charles and Diana sat together on a hay bale and talked. Diana told

Charles how sorry she was about his great-uncle. Diana told Charles that she thought he looked lonely and needed someone to look after him. Charles agreed.

Charles was taken with Diana. He thought she was pretty and fun. Diana was caring and even though she was just nineteen years old, Charles thought they had a lot in common. Charles's family liked her too and thought the pair would make a good match. In February 1981, Charles asked Diana to marry him, and she said yes.

"I'M DELIGHTED AND FRANKLY AMAZED THAT DIANA IS PREPARED TO TAKE ME ON."

Charles, Prince of Wales

News of the engagement caused a lot of excitement. A crowd gathered outside Buckingham Palace to celebrate the news, where the Coldstream Guards played the song "Congratulations". The prime minister congratulated the couple in parliament.

Shortly before the engagement, Diana had moved out of the flat she shared with her friends and into Clarence House where she could escape from the reporters who had followed her wherever she went ever since she had started seeing Charles. After the engagement was announced, she moved into Buckingham Palace.

Charles did not join her. Instead he continued with his schedule of royal visits, which included a tour in Australia and New Zealand.

Diana found life in Buckingham Palace lonely. She had hoped to spend time with her future husband, but he was away. Diana was left to face the pressure of royal wedding preparations by herself. She became depressed and developed an eating disorder.

When Charles returned from his tour, he was shocked by the change he saw in Diana. His 'jolly' young fiancée was moody and sad and had lost a lot of weight. Charles thought that Diana was suffering due to the stress of the wedding, and because she was adjusting to royal life. Charles hoped that once they were married, Diana would feel better.

A Fairy-Tale Wedding

Charles and Diana's wedding was billed to be the wedding of the year, attended not only by the couple's friends and family, but by world leaders, and watched by millions on televisions across the globe. As the palace prepared, newspapers ran stories speculating about every aspect of the day. Who would design the wedding dress? What kind of cake would they have? How many bridesmaids would there be? As excitement grew, shops cashed in by selling royal wedding souvenirs. Everything was printed with the smiling faces of the royal couple, from bottle openers and tea towels to tins of shortbread.

On 29 July 1981, Charles, wearing his naval commander uniform, waited at the altar of St Paul's

Cathedral as Diana, accompanied by her father, walked down the aisle towards him. Diana looked like a fairy-tale princess in an ivory satin gown with a seven-metre-long train. It is estimated that over 600,000 well-wishers from around the country travelled to London to see the royal couple on their big day. Charles was moved to see the crowds of people wishing them well and felt as if the whole country was a guest at his wedding.

After the ceremony, the couple returned to Buckingham Palace for the reception where they, and several thousand guests, enjoyed not one, but twenty-seven wedding cakes.

Charles and Diana spent their honeymoon sailing around Italy and Greece aboard the Royal Yacht *Britannia* before flying to Scotland to spend two and a half months at Balmoral.

Charles and Diana's wedding

A NEW FAMILY

Charles had hoped that Diana would feel better after the wedding when she could relax into her new life. Sadly, this did not happen. At Balmoral, Diana was frustrated that Charles seemed to want to spend all his time fishing or talking to old friends, rather than be with her. Diana was also worried that Charles was still in love with his former girlfriend, Camilla. After Charles and Camilla had ended their romantic relationship, Camilla had married a man named Andrew Parker Bowles. Charles had been heartbroken, but the pair had remained good friends and spoke to each other regularly on the telephone.

The Couple on Tour

In October, Charles and Diana travelled to Wales to undertake their first tour together on the royal train. Everywhere they went, Charles and Diana were greeted by waving crowds, but they hadn't come to see Charles. "We want Diana!" they chanted when the royal couple arrived. Some were so overcome when they met her that they cried or found themselves unable to let go of her hand. Diana was young, pretty and fashionable, and people loved her, leaving Charles feeling dull and ignored. In Cardiff, Diana gave her first speech when she thanked the Welsh people and said how proud she was to be their princess.

Diana found her first engagements overwhelming and was exhausted when she climbed back on to the train. Diana also felt sick, but soon found out that this was because she was expecting a baby.

A Home for the Newlyweds

After the wedding, Charles and Diana's London home and offices were in Charles's apartments of Buckingham Palace, but in the winter of 1981 they moved into apartments in Kensington Palace. The apartments had twenty-four rooms, including bedrooms, reception rooms and offices.

There was also a nursery, which had a bedroom and a playroom decorated with animals from Beatrix Potter.

Charles and Diana spent their weekends at Highgrove. Diana used this time to design the inside of the house, and Charles continued his work in the garden and also leased a nearby farm.

Charles wanted both the garden and the farm to be organic and not use any artificial fertilizers or pesticides. He also wanted to use traditional farming methods. He brought in rare breeds of animals and helped lay the hedgerows.

For his children, Charles built a large tree house with a thatched roof at the top of an old holly tree, which he named Holyrood House after the royal palace in Edinburgh.

A New Prince

On 21 June 1982, Diana gave birth to William Arthur Philip Louis at 9.03 pm at St Mary's Hospital in London. Outside the hospital, a crowd gathered, calling to see Charles and find out more about the new prince. An hour after his son was born, Charles went out to greet them. While shaking their hands, one lady gave Charles an excited kiss. Unlike his own father, Charles was present for his son's birth.

New Parents

Both Charles and Diana wanted to be unlike their own parents in the way they cared for William. Charles wanted to spend more time with his son than his father had spent with him. Charles changed nappies and took charge of bath times while Diana soothed William herself when he cried. When Charles was a baby, his mother had left him in the care of his grandmother and his nannies when she went on tour, even when she was gone for many months. Charles didn't want to do the same.

The Family Down Under

In April 1983, when Charles and Diana set off to visit Australia and New Zealand, they took nine-month-old William with them. Everywhere they went, crowds cheered for Diana, chanting her name. At home, newspapers printed pictures of her shaking hands and talking to children. Reporters wrote about what she wore, what she said and what a wonderful mother she seemed, leaving little room for anything about Charles. Charles was proud of Diana, and how much people seemed to love her, but he was also jealous. Diana found it exhausting. Unlike Charles, she had not grown up attending these events, or with this level of interest in her life. Charles helped her to cope with it, giving her tips such as shaking only one in every fifteen hands held out to her, and showing her how to wave so that her arm didn't feel as though it would fall off.

Both Charles and Diana were glad they had brought William along with them so that they didn't miss seeing him learning to crawl.

When Charles and Diana returned to London, the palace and the queen were delighted with how well the tour had gone. A few weeks later, the royal couple flew to Canada and received a similar reception.

Three Become Four

On 15 September 1984, Diana gave birth to another prince, Henry Charles Albert David, or Harry as he was soon known to everyone, at St Mary's Hospital, London. After his birth, Charles cut back on his engagements to spend time with his family, because he didn't want to miss the things his parents had missed from his own childhood.

At home, Charles and Diana struggled to find things they had in common, other than their children. Charles enjoyed reading, painting, classical music and hunting with his friends. Diana preferred pop music, she liked dancing and she found his friends, who were much older than her, stuffy and boring.

Charles and Diana with their sons

In April 1985, Charles and Diana sailed on the Royal Yacht *Britannia* to Italy, on a seventeen-day tour. Charles enjoyed seeing the art and architecture, which did not interest Diana. While in Italy, Charles and Diana had an audience with Pope John Paul II, who blessed them. As on previous tours, crowds greeted them wherever they went, cheering for Diana. The Italians loved her sense of style, and the press wrote about how beautiful and friendly she was. Charles resented the attention Diana received. When onboard *Britannia*, Charles spent his time painting watercolours with an artist, John Ward, who he had brought along to record the trip. Diana found Charles's interest in art boring and didn't understand what he saw in it.

A Royal Father

While Charles did not find much joy in being married, he delighted in being a father. Charles and his family spent time both in London and at Highgrove. Charles liked taking long walks with his sons and teaching them to ride. They played in the garden with their Jack Russell, named Tigga, and up in the treehouse he had built for them.

In the autumn of 1985, Charles and Diana toured the United States of America, visiting with President Reagan in Washington before travelling to Virginia and Palm Beach, Florida. Diana was celebrated for her movie-star good looks and her skill on the dance floor when she danced with actor John Travolta at the White House. On the outside, Charles and Diana were a great team, attracting crowds of people and raising money for charities, but at home they were anything but.

Cracks in the Fairy Tale

Instead of growing together, Charles and Diana grew further and further apart. They argued a lot. Charles didn't know what more he could do. He believed he had worked hard at his marriage. He even gave up seeing many old friends that Diana didn't like, but nothing helped. Diana was unhappy and he was too.

By the end of 1986, Charles and Diana lived

very separate lives. Diana liked staying in London, whereas Charles was happiest at Highgrove. Charles also preferred travelling and carrying out his public duties alone. Without the crowds screaming for Diana, Charles felt his engagements and speeches got the attention they deserved.

Charles Speaks Out

Charles threw himself into his work. He did not want to be a royal who used his position to cut ribbons and present awards. Charles knew that when he, as Prince of Wales, spoke, people listened, whether they agreed with him or not. Charles wanted to use his voice to speak out about subjects he cared about.

As Prince of Wales, he was a patron of many charities and organizations. Part of the role of patron is to attend events and give speeches. In 1982, Charles used these speeches as an opportunity to talk about issues he cared about. In a speech to the British Medical Association, Charles spoke out about the organization failing to embrace alternative medicines such as herbal remedies and acupuncture. At an event for the Royal Institute of British Architects, Charles spoke out about modern architecture, believing many buildings built after the Second World War were ugly and conflicted with the older buildings that surrounded them. He believed that this lack of harmony in architecture contributed to a lack of harmony in society, and appealed to architects to design buildings that sat comfortably next to buildings that were already there.

Charles also spoke out against modern practices in farming and for animal welfare. In a speech at the Royal Agricultural College in Cirencester, Charles said that industrial pesticides and fertilizers damaged the environment. He called on the organization to investigate farming methods that were sustainable and used renewable resources. Charles implemented these methods on his own farms, and implored others to do the same.

While many people disagreed with Charles, his words had an effect. In healthcare, the British Medical Association ran studies into the role alternative medicine and traditional medical practices could play in patients' recovery. In architecture, designs for buildings that had previously been given the go-ahead were redrawn and eventually Charles set up his own Institute of Architecture – a charity that involved communities in planning and development. In agriculture, Charles was part of a movement that took organic farming and sustainable methods from an unusual idea to the mainstream. Today, foods labelled 'organic' and 'sustainable' can be found in every supermarket in the country.

Prince on Page and Screen

As well as speeches, Charles wrote books and took part in television programmes to share his views.

In 1988, Charles took part in a television documentary called *A Vision of Britain – A Personal View of Architecture*. In the documentary, and in a book published in 1989, Charles called on architects to design buildings in keeping with buildings that are already there, to preserve the character of British towns and cities and improve the lives of people in urban environments.

Charles cared about the natural environment too. In 1990, he gave a lecture at the Royal Botanic Gardens at Kew on behalf of the environmental organization Friends of the Earth. In his lecture, Charles called for the protection of the world's rainforests and the communities living within them.

"ONCE A RAINFOREST OR A SPECIES LIVING IN IT IS GONE, IT IS GONE FOR EVER. THE PHRASE 'NOW OR NEVER' HAS NEVER BEEN USED WITH MORE

CHILLING ACCURACY THAN WHEN APPLIED TO THE TASK OF SAVING THE REMAINING RAINFORESTS."

Charles, Prince of Wales

Charles's lecture was so well received, he published it as a book.

In his spare time, Charles continued to paint. He had been interested in art since his school days and took up watercolours shortly after leaving Cambridge. Charles took artists with him to record his travels and painted alongside them whenever he could. In 1991, a book of his own watercolour paintings was published. Profits from the sales of Charles's books went to the Prince of Wales's Charitable Foundation.

Charles used his television programmes and books as a way to express himself, and although he didn't know it, his wife was about to do the same.

Diana – The Bestseller

Diana worked with a journalist named Andrew Morton to help her tell her story. Morton's book, *Diana – Her True Story* was published in June 1992 and became an instant bestseller. In it, Morton claimed Diana was unhappy in her marriage. He revealed Diana's struggles with her mental health, the arguments she had with Charles, and how he was a distant husband and father. Morton also implied that Charles was in a romantic relationship with someone else: his ex-girlfriend Camilla Parker Bowles. Diana's book flew off the shelves and the press went wild publishing stories. It was only revealed later that Diana had helped to write the book.

Charles felt betrayed. Even though he and Diana lived separate lives by then, he had hoped they could be friendly to one another, to continue their work and protect their sons. In telling the world about their private life, Charles felt Diana had made that impossible. Charles was embarrassed in front of his family, and in front of the world.

On 9 December 1992, Prime Minister John Major declared in parliament:

"IT IS ANNOUNCED FROM BUCKINGHAM PALACE THAT, WITH REGRET, THE PRINCE AND PRINCESS OF WALES HAVE DECIDED TO SEPARATE."

Prime Minister John Major

The prime minister added that although they were separating, the royal couple had no plans to divorce.

An Unpopular Prince

From the beginning of their marriage, the public loved Diana in a way they had never loved Charles. At engagements, Diana was seen as warm and sympathetic, whereas Charles was business-like. As a mother, Diana kissed and hugged William and Harry in public, whereas Charles had been brought up to behave more formally in front of the cameras. After reading Diana's story, people were angry with Charles for having caused her so much pain. They believed that when he betrayed her, he betrayed them too. Many people were on Diana's side.

A Royal Mess

Although they both continued to carry out royal duties, some members of the government and the Church of England believed that Charles's behaviour and the failure of his marriage meant that he was no longer a fit heir to the throne. If, and when, Charles became king, he would also become Defender of the Faith and Supreme

Governor of the Church of England and promise to uphold the laws of the Anglican Church. They believed that in breaking the vows of his marriage, Charles had broken these laws.

They believed the royal family should set an example to the rest of the country, but the example Charles and other members of the royal family were setting was not one they wanted people to follow.

Charles's wasn't the only royal marriage that was in trouble. Charles's sister, Princess Anne, had announced her separation from her husband, Captain Mark Phillips, in 1989 and divorced in 1992. And, after six years of marriage, Charles's brother Andrew announced his separation from wife, Sarah. People were more interested in the royal family than ever before, but it was for all the wrong reasons.

The Interviews

Charles was frustrated. Despite his hard work, the years of service, hundreds of speeches, many thousands of engagements, long hours of travel and the success of his charitable organizations, the only stories the press were interested in publishing about him were about his marriage. And they only had one side of the story, Diana's.

In June 1994, twenty-five years after his investiture as Prince of Wales, Charles took part in a television interview and worked on a biography with a journalist named Jonathan Dimbleby. Charles wanted to tell his story. Not only about his marriage, but about who he was: his life, his work and his vision for the monarchy. Charles also talked about his experiences growing up, his family and his marriage, and confessed that once he believed his marriage was over, he began a romantic relationship with Camilla Parker Bowles.

In November the following year, Diana took part in her own interview with journalist Martin Bashir, once again revealing her unhappiness and how she believed their marriage was over, once and for all.

A Royal Divorce

Once again, the Prince and Princess of Wales were on the front pages. Keen for the scandal to end sooner rather than later, the palace announced that the queen had written to both Charles and Diana, urging them to divorce as soon as possible. On 15 July 1996, Charles and Diana's fifteen-year marriage was over.

Charles and Diana agreed to share the responsibilities of looking after their sons. During their separation, Charles and Diana had tried to hide their disagreements from William and Harry, and to protect them from the stories in the papers and on television. Charles hoped that, now the divorce was final, he and Diana could work out how to move forward as a new family.

Tragically that wasn't to be.

A SINGLE PARENT

Charles and Diana agreed when they divorced that their sons, William and Harry, would split their holidays between them. In 1997, William and Harry spent part of their summer holiday with their mother Diana in the South of France, on a yacht owned by her friend Dodi al Fayed's family, before spending a month with their father and the royal family at Balmoral.

Shocking News

In the very early morning of 31 August 1997, Charles received news that would change all of their lives for ever. Diana, Princess of Wales had died in a car accident in Paris.

Charles didn't know what to do, but he wanted to protect his sons from the news for as long as he could. Rather than wake them, Charles let them sleep, and removed the television from their sitting room.

When they woke, Charles told William and Harry that their mother had been in an accident and had died. Later, Charles spoke to his parents and his advisors, and they agreed that Charles would travel to Paris to accompany Diana's body home, while William and Harry would stay at Balmoral with the family until the funeral.

At Balmoral, Elizabeth and Philip looked after the boys and comforted them. They took them on walks and picnics and kept them away from the newspapers and television. They also kept them away from the press and the public.

Many people in the United Kingdom and around the world had loved Diana and were devastated by her death. Thousands of people travelled to London to leave flowers outside her home at Kensington Palace as well as outside Buckingham Palace.

The Prince Wore Blue

On 6 September, one week after receiving the tragic news, Charles and the boys got ready for the funeral. While William and Harry wore traditional black suits, Charles wore blue as a tribute to his late wife, who had told him she liked him best in that colour. In the royal family it is a tradition for close family members to walk behind their loved one's coffin as part of the procession to Westminster Abbey. Even though William and Harry were just fifteen and twelve years old respectively, Charles believed they should do the same.

What Happens Next?

After the funeral, Charles stayed at Highgrove House with his sons for two weeks before they returned to school. The princes' lives would look very different, and they needed to work out how to move forward as a family of three.

When Charles returned to his public duties, he worried that the public would blame him for Diana's death, but they did not. When Charles appeared at engagements, they were kind and supportive and asked him how he and his sons were coping with the loss. Charles was touched.

The Boys on Tour

In order to spend more time with his boys, Charles began to include them in his working life. In November 1997, Charles took Harry with him on an official visit to South Africa. At a state dinner hosted by Nelson Mandela, President of South Africa, Charles took the opportunity to give his thanks for all of the condolences he and his sons had received since Diana's death, and how it proved how much she had meant to people.

NELSON MANDELA

Nelson Mandela was born in South Africa in 1918 while the country was governed by white South Africans who believed in a racist system known as 'apartheid'. Apartheid gave all the power to white South Africans and restricted where Black people could live and work and what jobs they were allowed to do. Nelson, like many people in South Africa thought this was unfair.

While at university, Nelson met other people who thought the system was unfair and who wanted to change things. Nelson became a leader of a group of activists who protested against apartheid. When the government did not listen to their protests, Nelson and his group of activists bombed property to get people's attention.

It worked. The South African government took notice of what they were doing, but they did not want to end apartheid or give up their power. In 1964, Nelson was arrested and sentenced to life in prison, but this wasn't the end of his fight. Nelson and his group of activists had captured the attention of activists around the world who put pressure on their leaders to put pressure on South Africa to end apartheid and free Nelson Mandela. This pressure included limiting trade with South Africa and not allowing them to enter teams in sporting competitions.

Nelson Mandela was released from prison in 1990 and continued his campaign against apartheid and for free elections in South Africa. In April 1994, South Africa had its first general election in which citizens of all races were allowed to vote. When the votes were counted, the party led by Nelson Mandela, called the African National Congress (ANC), won.

After serving as president, Nelson Mandela continued to fight against injustice in South Africa and around the world.

At the end of their trip, Charles hosted a benefit concert in Johannesburg in aid of the Prince's Trust and introduced Harry to the stars of the show, the Spice Girls.

In March 1998, Charles took William and Harry to Canada to combine both work and fun. When they arrived in Vancouver, Charles realized that his sons weren't little boys any more. Fifteen-year-old William was greeted by thousands of screaming fans waving flowers and wanting to shake his hand. Back at home, the press referred to the reception as 'Wills Mania'.

After visiting a school in Vancouver, Charles took his sons away from the frenzy to ski in the mountains in Whistler, but some of the frenzy followed.

Charles and the palace had made it clear that this part of the trip was a private holiday and that they were not to be disturbed, but a Canadian television crew filmed them at a ski lift. Charles was annoyed and the Canadian government issued a statement, warning that if the incident was repeated, the journalists involved could have their press credentials revoked.

Charles was protective of his sons. When he was growing up, it bothered him when the press followed his every move, and it was worse for William and Harry. Independent photographers, known as paparazzi, contributed to the accident that killed their mother as they chased her car. Diana's car crashed while travelling at high speed to escape from photographers on motorcycles.

Blending Families

After his divorce, Charles had planned to introduce Camilla to William and Harry, but after Diana died, they decided to wait. Charles and Camilla were very much in love and saw each other whenever they could but were careful to make sure Charles's sons were elsewhere when she visited Highgrove.

Charles with William and Harry

Charles worried William and Harry blamed Camilla for their parents' divorce and wasn't sure how they would get along with her and her two children. But if Camilla was going to remain a part of his life, Charles would have to find out.

Charles was pleased when they all seemed to get along and Camilla and her children became part of Charles's family.

In the summer of 1998, William met Camilla at St James's Palace. Camilla was nervous, but William soon got her talking about polo and horses. Charles and Camilla were relieved. William met Camilla twice more before Harry began to join them.

Looking Ahead

In November 1998, Charles celebrated his fiftieth birthday with not one but seven birthday parties.

As part of Charles's birthday celebrations, a television programme called *Charles at 50* was produced, in which the prince talked about the future of the monarchy. Charles believed the way the monarchy worked needed updating to fit with the modern world.

Charles proposed that, in the future, the royal family should fund itself using money from the Crown Estate (see page 62) and not receive money from the government. Charles wanted to open up Buckingham Palace as a museum where he would display art from the Royal Collection. He also believed that there should be fewer working royals.

Charles's mother and father threw Charles a party at Buckingham Palace. The guests included the prime minister and representatives from the prince's many charities. At the party, Charles thanked his parents for having put up with him since 1948.

On 14 November, Camilla hosted a party for Charles at Highgrove. William and Harry were invited, as were many of Charles's friends, but Charles's parents did not attend. The queen did not think it was appropriate for them to be seen at the same events, but her sister Princess Margaret went.

PRINCESS MARGARET

When Princess Margaret was in her twenties, she fell in love with a man named Captain Peter Townsend, who had worked for her father, King George VI. Princess Margaret and Captain Peter Townsend intended to marry, but there was a problem. Captain Peter Townsend had been married before and was divorced. At this time, the Church of England did not allow divorced people to marry in a church if their previous partners were still alive. Queen Elizabeth and the UK government would not let Margaret marry. Left with no choice, Margaret and Peter went their separate ways, and married other people, but Margaret never forgot how it felt for her love not to be accepted by the palace.

In 2002, Charles said goodbye to two very important figures in his life. On 9 February 2002, his aunt Princess Margaret died. Princess Margaret had listened to Charles and supported him throughout his life.

On 30 March 2002, Charles's beloved grandmother died at her home at Royal Lodge, Windsor. The

Queen Mother was 101 years of age when she died. Charles loved his grandmother very much. She had looked after him when he was little, when his mother was away on tour, and she had listened to him complain about school. Charles said the Queen Mother always saw the funny side of life and that her home was always full of laughter and love.

"FOR ME, SHE MEANT EVERYTHING AND I HAD DREADED, DREADED THIS MOMENT ALONG WITH, I KNOW, COUNTLESS OTHERS. SOMEHOW, I NEVER THOUGHT IT WOULD COME."

Charles, Prince of Wales

Charles with Queen Elizabeth II

A Golden Celebration

Three months after the death of his grandmother, Charles helped lead the celebrations of his mother's Golden Jubilee marking fifty years since she became queen. To mark the occasion, Buckingham Palace threw open the gates to its garden to host a pop concert, featuring artists such as Shirley Bassey and Elton John. At the end of the concert Charles thanked his mother for allowing the concert which helped him to raise a lot of money for charity, and praised her for being:

"...A BEACON OF TRADITION AND STABILITY IN THE MIDST OF PROFOUND, SOMETIMES PERILOUS CHANGE."

Charles, Prince of Wales

But not all the changes were perilous; some were good, and one took place on Charles's birthday.

A Change of Heart

On 14 November 2002, a spokesperson for the Church of England announced that from then on they would allow divorced people to remarry within the church. They said that this would be in exceptional circumstances only, but that the Church believed that if God could "forgive and make possible fresh starts", then so should they.

A Fresh Start

Charles longed to marry Camilla, but it would take time. The British public had loved Diana, and they needed time to get to know Camilla and to adjust to the idea of him marrying again, as did his family. Charles introduced Camilla to his mother and father and the rest of his family. Camilla loved horses and hunting and was devoted to Charles so eventually everyone came to accept her.

In 2004, Charles consulted with the archbishop of Canterbury to see if he and Camilla would be allowed to marry within the Anglican Church. Unfortunately, because Charles and Camilla's romantic relationship had contributed to the breakdown of their marriages, the Archbishop said they would not. He added, however, that he saw no reason why Charles could not marry Camilla in a civil ceremony and have the marriage blessed by a minister. It was not the answer Charles was looking for, but it was enough.

As heir to the throne, Charles also had to have permission from his mother, who gave it happily. William and Harry also gave their blessing.

Charles proposed to Camilla in December 2004, and she said yes.

A Small Ceremony and One Big Party

On 9 April 2005, Charles, Prince of Wales married Camilla Parker Bowles at Windsor Guildhall surrounded by just twenty-eight guests. After the ceremony, the couple travelled to St George's Chapel, Windsor to have their marriage blessed in front of 800 guests including Queen Elizabeth and Prince Philip.

Charles and Camilla at their wedding

"I'M VERY PROUD AND WISH THEM WELL. MY SON IS HOME AND DRY WITH THE WOMAN HE LOVES."

Queen Elizabeth II

As a mark of respect for Princess Diana, it was decided that after the wedding, rather than taking the title 'Princess of Wales', Camilla would become the Duchess of Cornwall. It was also decided that when Charles became king, Camilla, as his second wife, would become Princess Consort instead of Queen Consort.

Charles and Camilla spent their honeymoon painting, fishing and walking at Balmoral Estate in Scotland, a quiet escape before beginning her life as a royal. As Charles and Camilla were starting their lives as newlyweds, Charles's sons were also starting new lives of their own.

THE NEXT GENERATION

When choosing schools for William and Harry, Charles's main concern was that they both had a better time than he did, and in this he succeeded.

William was the first heir to the throne to attend nursery school when he was three years old. After nursery, both William and Harry attended a private day school in London. Charles had been driven to school each day by a chauffeur, whereas Diana took William and Harry to school whenever she could and was there to meet them at the end of the day. When William turned eight years old, he attended Ludgrove School, a boarding school in Wokingham, Berkshire, where he became captain of the rugby team.

William started Eton College when he was thirteen. Charles had wanted to attend Eton College himself when he was a boy, to be closer to Windsor. For Diana, her father and brother had gone there, which meant Diana was familiar with the school and felt comfortable sending her boys there. William's first day in 1995 was a family event. Despite their differences, Charles and Diana both attended and brought Harry along too so that he could get to know the place for when it was his turn.

When William started school, Charles and the palace made an agreement with the major newspapers that the princes should be left alone. Unlike Charles, who had stories about his pocket money make international headlines, and his stolen essays featured in magazines, tales about his sons' schooldays did not make the news.

School sheltered William and Harry from news stories about their parents too. Teachers at both Ludgrove and Eton did their best to keep the boys away from the papers and asked their parents to warn them when big stories, such as the interviews, were going to break so that the boys weren't taken by surprise.

Being away from home was hard at times on both of the boys, especially after their mother's death, but thankfully, both Ludgrove School and Eton College were just a short drive away from Windsor Castle where they could spend time with family. In 1998, Harry joined William at Eton, where they were able to look out for one another.

After completing his A-levels, William went on to study geography at the University of St Andrews in Scotland. Before arriving at university, the palace made another agreement with the press to leave William alone to study. This agreement, and the fact that St Andrews was so far from London, made it easier for William to live like other students. William even managed to find a girlfriend, named Catherine Middleton. William and Catherine met in their first year and soon became close. By William's third year at St Andrews, Catherine had met William's family and was invited on holidays with Charles and Harry. William graduated from university in 2005.

Harry left Eton College in 2003 after completing his A-levels, but did not follow his brother to university. Instead Harry wanted to join the army. After taking some time out of studying to travel, in May 2005 Harry began studying at the Royal Military Academy Sandhurst.

No Idle Prince

With his marriage settled, and his children happily getting on with their own lives, Charles was able to get on with his work.

By 2005, Charles's office ran seventeen charities, for which he raised more than one hundred million pounds a year. The prince's charities tackled various issues, from providing young people with support in pursuing their careers to a scheme rolled out in countries around the world that promoted and protected traditional crafts. All of the prince's charities worked towards the same goal of creating a more sustainable world by encouraging and supporting people to learn new skills and cooperate with one another.

THE PRINCE'S TRUST

The Prince's Trust is a charity set up by Prince Charles in 1976 to help provide young people from disadvantaged backgrounds with opportunities to improve their lives. The first projects funded by the Prince's Trust included providing young people in Cornwall with free training to become certified lifeguards and funding a fishing club set up by two young men with criminal records. The Prince's Trust raises money by hosting rock music galas featuring artists such as Kate Bush and Beyoncé. The Prince's Trust uses the money it raises to give young people access to free courses, grants and mentoring. Courses offered by the Prince's Trust help young people discover their potential, gain qualifications and learn the skills they need to find work. Since it began, the Prince's Trust has joined forces with businesses such as TK Maxx and organizations such as the Professional Football Association to help young people start their careers. Grants from the Prince's Trust can be used to pay for training or to set up a business. These grants have helped more than 90,000 young people set up their own businesses.

It is estimated that the Prince's Trust has helped more than 1 million young people get started in fields as varied as professional sports and entertainment to construction and retail.

Following its success in the United Kingdom, the Prince's Trust set up similar initiatives in Canada, New Zealand, Australia and the USA.

As Prince of Wales, Charles often worked seven days a week, starting soon after breakfast and often continuing until late into the night. He was disciplined and had high standards for himself, and expected the same from the people he worked with.

Being a royal meant that he met lots of people and Charles was good at connecting people and motivating them to work together to solve problems.

"SUCCESS BREEDS SUCCESS, AND ONCE YOU SHOW PEOPLE WHAT YOU ARE DOING, IT'S AMAZING HOW THEY WANT TO GO ON HELPING."

Charles, Prince of Wales

As well as running his own charities, Charles was patron of hundreds of other organizations. These included charities, such as the Wildfowl and Wetlands Trust and the Soil Association, and professional societies such as the Specialist Cheesemakers Association.

Charles and the Environment

One of the causes Charles has championed throughout his life is caring for the environment. He made his first speech about the environment in 1970 when he talked about the dangers posed by the increased use of plastics. When Charles first voiced his concern for the environment, it was not a mainstream topic of conversation. Many people thought he was mad, but today, more people understand the importance of caring about the planet we live on and understand the danger of failing to change our behaviour. Since then, Charles has given speeches and lectures about global warming, deforestation, pollution, the damage done by unsustainable farming and business practices, the benefits of recycling and the preservation of endangered species and ecosystems. Charles has even spoken about the small changes people can make that can have a big impact on the planet, such as turning off lights.

Charles tried to live more sustainably too. He had his car converted to run on a mix of surplus wine and whey left over from cheese production and he had the royal train's engine adapted to run on used cooking oil. On family holidays, Charles would take his sons litter picking through the countryside, filling bags with rubbish people had left behind. At school, Harry was teased for doing it, because he thought it was what everyone did when they went on a walk.

"WITH CLIMATE CHANGE, WE ARE RUNNING OUT OF TIME BECAUSE THE NECESSARY ACTION HASN'T BEEN TAKEN."

Charles, Prince of Wales

In January 2007, Charles was awarded the Global Environmental Citizen Award by Harvard Medical School's Centre for Health and the Global Environment. This award is presented each year to people who do outstanding work towards protecting the global environment. Previous winners included former US Vice President Al Gore and scientist and conservationist Dame Jane Goodall.

"I HAVE ALWAYS BEEN IMPRESSED BY HIS ABILITY TO UNDERSTAND COMPLEX GLOBAL ISSUES AND HIS DEEP COMMITMENT TO SOLVE THE PRESSING ISSUES FACING OUR WORLD."

Former US Vice President Al Gore

During the ceremony, Charles was praised for his lifelong commitment to environmental causes, both within his own network of charities, and with many of the charities he represented. He was also commended for his work pioneering organic and sustainable farming practices with the Duchy's Original food company he started in 1990.

Building Communities

As well as working to protect the global environment, Charles was also interested in bringing new life to local environments. In 2007, Charles bought a large house in Scotland named Dumfries House. The house had fallen into disrepair and needed a lot of work to restore it. The community around Dumfries House needed help too. The area had once been a prosperous coal-mining community. During the 1980s the mines closed. Many in the community left to find work. Those who stayed struggled to find employment.

Charles decided to buy land that surrounded

Dumfries House and build an estate to provide people with work. He set up courses to train people in skills such as textiles, engineering, farming and catering. Using money raised by the estate, Charles paid to refurbish the community town hall and open-air swimming pool. Within the grounds of the estate, Charles built a sports centre and a health clinic. He also set up a sustainable farm. Charles and his team worked hard to transform Dumfries House into the second largest employer in the area, providing care and training for the people living nearby.

Putting Pen to Paper

When Charles celebrated his sixtieth birthday in 2008, he said he was, "one of those people who minds a lot about things." Over the years, Charles has minded and been bothered about a lot of different issues, from architecture to youth unemployment, and even road layout. But Charles didn't let being bothered worry him, though some people might have thought it did a bit.

The Black Spider Memos

Charles said some of the ways he kept his sanity were "gardening, walking and writing letters." Charles wrote a lot of letters to lots of politicians. Even though some the people Charles wrote to received thousands of letters, they didn't receive many from princes.

When twenty-seven of Charles's letters were printed in the newspapers, they were nicknamed the 'Black Spider Memos' because of his scratchy black handwriting. Some of the letters were addressed to Prime Minister Tony Blair and members of his cabinet. Some people criticized Charles for attempting to influence members of the government and accused him of 'meddling'. They believed that as future king, he should remain neutral, but Charles didn't agree. As heir to the throne, rather than the monarch, Charles felt it was his duty to get involved, and use the limited power he had to draw attention to causes that were being ignored.

"IF THAT'S CALLED MEDDLING, I'M VERY PROUD OF IT."

Charles, Prince of Wales

One of the reasons Charles felt it was so important to get involved with issues such as helping young people, or preserving the environment, was because he wanted things to get better for people living now and for future generations.

"I DON'T WANT TO BE CONFRONTED BY MY FUTURE GRANDCHILD AND THEM SAY, 'WHY DIDN'T YOU DO SOMETHING?'"

Charles, Prince of Wales

William Weds

On 29 April 2011, Prince William married Catherine Middleton at Westminster Abbey. William proposed using the ring Charles had given his mother, Diana, thirty years before, and just like his wedding to Diana, the world watched the young couple on their big day. But aside from that, things were different for William and Kate.

William and Catherine
at their wedding

William had known Catherine for a long time. Unlike Diana, Catherine had had the chance to think long and hard about what she was getting into by marrying the heir to the throne. It was not a future she had been raised to expect, for while Catherine had come from a wealthy family, she had not come from a 'noble' family. Rather than manage a grand house and an estate, Catherine's family ran a successful party supply company.

William and Catherine even lived together before they were married, sharing a house on the island of Anglesey, in Wales, from 2010. William and Catherine lived in Wales while William completed his training with the Royal Air Force. After the wedding, the Duke and Duchess of Cambridge returned to their house, and four days after his wedding, William went back to work as a search and rescue pilot.

Brothers in Arms

From 2006, while William served in the Royal Air Force, Harry served in the army. In 2012, Harry travelled to Afghanistan to serve with the

Army Air Corps as a helicopter pilot and gunner. It was Harry's second tour in Afghanistan, having served there in 2007 with the Blues and Royals regiment.

Charles was proud of his son, but he also worried about him. The war in Afghanistan took place from 2001 to 2014 and claimed the lives of more than 450 British military personnel.

"IF YOU ARE A PARENT ... OR A LOVED ONE AND THE PERSON YOU LOVE IS AWAY LIKE THAT, IN THESE INCREDIBLY DANGEROUS CIRCUMSTANCES, I KNOW

YOU WORRY ALL THE TIME. CERTAINLY EVERY NIGHT WHEN I GO TO BED I WORRY."

Charles, Prince of Wales

Charles knew just how dangerous the circumstances were first-hand, after visiting some of the 9,500 British troops serving in Afghanistan in 2010. Charles said he made the visit because he wanted to show his support and say thank you.

THE WAR IN AFGHANISTAN

On 11 September 2001, nineteen men hijacked four passenger aircraft and used them to attack targets in the United States. Two aircraft crashed into the twin towers of the

World Trade Center in New York City, one crashed into the Pentagon in Washington DC and the fourth crashed in Pennsylvania. The attack claimed the lives of nearly 3,000 people. A terrorist organization named al-Qaeda claimed responsibility for the attack.

The men who hijacked the aircraft had all trained in Afghanistan and the US believed that the leaders of al-Qaeda were based there and supported by the Taliban, the government in Afghanistan. In October 2001, the US and their ally, the United Kingdom, entered Afghanistan to fight al-Qaeda and the Taliban. Although the Taliban regime quickly fell in November 2001, its forces continued to cause problems and the region was very unstable for many years. The founder of al-Qaeda, Osama bin Laden, was killed by US forces in 2011. The USA and the North Atlantic Treaty Organization (NATO) withdrew from Afghanistan in 2021.

A Proud Grandfather

Throughout his life, Charles has been awarded many titles and patronages but one of the titles he is most proud of is 'grandfather'.

On 22 July 2013, the palace announced that Catherine, Duchess of Cambridge had given birth to a little boy – Prince George Alexander Louis, at St Mary's Hospital, London. As the first-born son of Prince William, who was second in line to the throne, Prince George replaced Prince Harry as third in line. He was also Prince Charles's first grandchild. Charles couldn't wait to meet the newest member of the family.

"GRANDPARENTHOOD IS A UNIQUE MOMENT IN ANYONE'S LIFE, AS COUNTLESS KIND

PEOPLE HAVE TOLD ME IN RECENT MONTHS, SO I AM ENORMOUSLY PROUD AND HAPPY TO BE A GRANDFATHER FOR THE FIRST TIME AND WE ARE EAGERLY LOOKING FORWARD TO SEEING THE BABY IN THE NEAR FUTURE."

Charles, Prince of Wales

After George was born, Charles planted an arboretum to honour him at Birkhall, his home in Aberdeenshire. Charles called the arboretum "Prince George's Wood".

As George grew up, Charles liked to read him stories such as the *Harry Potter* books by J.K. Rowling, even doing all the voices.

On 2 May 2015, the Duke and Duchess of Cambridge had a daughter, Princess Charlotte Elizabeth Diana – Charles's second grandchild. William and Catherine named their little girl after her grandfather, her great-grandmother and her grandmother. In April 2018, George and Charlotte were joined by a younger brother: Prince Louis Arthur Charles.

Prince William was pleased with how his father took to the role of grandfather and thought he was brilliant at it. Charles's only wish was that he had more time to spend with his grandchildren. But Charles had less time than ever before.

Prince George, Princess Charlotte and Prince Louis

Slowing Down

In September 2015, Queen Elizabeth II became Great Britain's longest serving monarch, beating the record set by her great-great-grandmother, Queen Victoria, who reigned for sixty-three years, seven months and two days. In April the following year, the queen celebrated her ninetieth birthday, with a series of parties and parades in her honour.

"AS WE CELEBRATE HER NINETIETH BIRTHDAY, SHE, LIKE ALL OF US, CAN REFLECT ON A LIFE THAT HAS INSPIRED AND

ENCOURAGED MILLIONS OF PEOPLE IN THE UNITED KINGDOM, THE COMMONWEALTH AND AROUND THE WORLD."

Charles, Prince of Wales

But Charles's parents were getting older. The retirement age for women in the United Kingdom in 2016 was sixty-five years old, but the queen was very much a working royal. She attended events and was able to perform many of her duties, but there were some things she couldn't do. Charles's father, Prince Philip, at ninety-six years old had started to pull back too. Prince Philip had been fit and healthy all of his life and prided himself on his ability to keep going, but in 2017 the palace announced that after serving the country for more than seventy years, Prince Philip was retiring from public life.

Stepping Up

In 2011, Prince Charles took on many of his father's patronages including that of President of the Worldwide Fund for Nature. Charles also filled in for his mother at public events and on tours, but he couldn't do everything. Thankfully, his family were close at hand. Prince William finished serving with the Royal Air Force in 2017 and moved to Kensington Palace with his family. William and Catherine took on some of Queen Elizabeth's and Prince Philip's patronages as well as new ones of their own.

Prince Harry was on hand to help, too. In 2015, Prince Harry left the army after ten years of service to begin his life as working royal. Prince Harry became involved in a number of military charities as well as working with William and Catherine to raise awareness of and help people have conversations about their mental health.

Passing the Torch

....

The queen believed that some roles were suited to Charles alone. When Elizabeth became queen in 1952, she also took on the role of Head of the Commonwealth of Nations. Since then, the organization had grown from eight to fifty-four member countries, to which Elizabeth had made nearly two hundred visits, and held regular audiences with their leaders. In 2018, Elizabeth invited leaders from within the commonwealth to London and Windsor for the annual Commonwealth Heads of Government Meeting (CHOGM). As well as discussing issues such as climate change, extremism and online security, this meeting had another important item on the agenda – who would become the next head of the commonwealth? Unable to make long flights as she used to, Elizabeth called on them to elect a new leader to take her place. The role of Head of the Commonwealth would not pass to Charles automatically, but Elizabeth said it was her "sincerest wish" for him to be given the opportunity to continue her work. At the closing press conference, it was announced that upon the queen's death, the next Head of the Commonwealth would be Charles, Prince of Wales. Charles had supported his mother's work with the commonwealth for more than forty years. UK Prime Minister Theresa May said the vote had been unanimous.

When Harry Met Meghan

With William happily married, Harry was left to face the intense curiosity of the British press alone. News organizations wound themselves into a frenzy with predictions as to who would marry Great Britain's 'most eligible bachelor', just as they had with Charles forty years before. Harry was in no hurry to decide, until 2016, when a friend introduced him to an American actor named Meghan Markle. Harry and Meghan liked each other immediately, and after a whirlwind romance of little over a year, Clarence House announced that the couple were engaged and planned to marry in the spring of 2018. Charles was thrilled to welcome

Meghan into the family.

Even though Harry was all grown up, he still needed his dad's help. Shortly before the big day, Harry confided in Charles that Meghan's father was unable to make the wedding. Harry asked if he would walk Meghan down the aisle instead.

Charles walks Meghan down the aisle

Charles didn't hesitate. On 19 May 2018, Prince Charles walked Meghan Markle down the aisle at St George's Chapel, Windsor, before taking a seat for a service that included the traditions of both his son and his future daughter-in-law – a sermon given by US Reverend Michael Curry, the chief pastor of the Episcopal Church and a ceremony conducted by the archbishop of Canterbury, Justin Welby.

As well as being a beautiful wedding, it was also a historic one because Meghan was the first non-white, bi-racial person to marry into the royal family. Meghan's mother, Doria Ragland, a yoga teacher and make-up artist, was Black and her father, Thomas Markle, was white. Meghan was also an American; she grew up in Los Angeles, California. Meghan had been married (and divorced) before. In 1936, Edward VIII gave up the throne to marry Wallis Simpson, an American divorcee (see page 27), but changes within the Church and public opinion meant Harry could marry Meghan without having to give up anything, yet.

Momentous Milestones

Shortly after the wedding, on 22 May, Charles attended a garden party held in his honour at

Buckingham Palace. Harry and Meghan, now the Duke and Duchess of Sussex, delayed their honeymoon to attend. Also at the party were 6,000 representatives from the many charities Charles served. The garden party was the first of many events celebrating Charles's seventieth birthday. Charles's birthday celebrations included a magic show at the London Palladium, a gala concert at Buckingham Palace and a tea party with seventy inspirational guests also turning seventy that year. The guests were voted for by the charity AgeUK.

A Long-term Investment

In March 2019, Charles and his family had gathered at a reception to celebrate fifty years since his investiture as Prince of Wales. The reception was held at Buckingham Palace. Representatives from Charles's Welsh charities and prominent figures from Wales and elsewhere in the United Kingdom were invited. After his investiture in 1969, Charles had continued his relationship with Wales, visiting regularly and setting up charities to serve the community.

Charles owned a house in Carmarthenshire, Wales, where he had spent a lot of time. He became a member of the local community and helped to maintain buildings in the village. Charles wanted his home in Wales to become a showcase for heritage crafts. Far from being someone who wanted to repress Welsh culture, Charles had done everything he could to preserve it.

When Charles was invested as Prince of Wales, many in Wales were against him. How did they feel fifty years on? Dafydd Iwan, who wrote and performed the Welsh Nationalist folk song 'Carlo', felt Charles had, "done the best of a bad job."

"THERE'S NO POINT IN PAINTING HIM AS AN EVIL CHARACTER. I THINK HE HAS DONE SOME

EXCELLENT WORK THROUGH THE PRINCE'S TRUST ... HE HAS CONTRIBUTED, YES."

Dafydd Iwan

To celebrate Charles's seventieth birthday, the palace released a picture of Charles, taken at Clarence House. In the picture Charles smiled happily, surrounded by his growing family. Charles and his family had overcome many challenges to be together.

TURBULENT TIMES

On 6 May 2019, Charles celebrated the birth of his fourth grandchild. Archie Harrison Mountbatten-Windsor was born at the Portland Hospital in London. On 16 May, Charles travelled to Windsor to visit Archie and his parents, Meghan and Harry, at their home, Frogmore Cottage. It was a happy moment in a year that had often been far from it for Meghan and Harry.

A Racist Reception

The wedding of Prince Harry and Meghan was a historic moment for the royal family. Many people in the United Kingdom and around the world delighted in the fact that the royal family was becoming more diverse, and more representative of the country and the commonwealth. Others were not so happy. Some of the British media said bigoted things about Meghan's background; others made racist comments about their son Archie, comparing him to a monkey. In an interview in 2021, Meghan claimed some of these racist comments came from members of the royal family itself.

As well as racist comments, Meghan was made the subject of hundreds of news articles which painted her as difficult and demanding, and compared her unfavourably with her sister-in-law, the Duchess of Cambridge.

Harry struggled watching his wife suffer and was angry about how the press treated her. He was frightened too. Harry was scared that the merciless media attention would end in a tragedy similar to the one that killed his mother, Diana.

Prince Charles and Camilla, Duchess of Cornwall, celebrated Christmas in 2019 with the queen, Prince Philip, the Duke and Duchess of Cambridge and the three grandchildren. It was a traditional

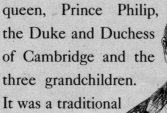

royal family Christmas, but the Duke and Duchess of Sussex and Archie were not there.

A Royal Split

On 8 January 2020, Prince Harry announced that he and his wife Meghan were stepping down as working members of the royal family and relocating their family to the United States where they wanted to work. Charles was heartbroken that his son had chosen to leave the family. He had hoped that they could work together to come up with another solution. Sadly, that wasn't to be. Later, in an interview, Prince Harry said he made the decision to protect his family.

As difficult as the news was, worse was soon to follow. News that would affect not just the royal family, but millions of families all over the world.

THE COVID-19 PANDEMIC

In January 2020, the news was dominated by stories of a new virus that was first discovered in Wuhan, China. This virus was named COVID-19 and was spreading quickly through Asia and Europe. The symptoms of COVID-19 included a cough, fever, and a loss of taste and smell. Some people infected with COVID-19 had no symptoms at all, whereas others became gravely ill, and many died. The worst symptoms were experienced by people over sixty years old, and people who had health conditions that made them more vulnerable to infection.

Day after day, more and more people became infected with the virus. Hospitals were in danger of being overwhelmed, with medical staff getting sick too. To ease the pressure, governments around the world closed businesses and schools, implementing lockdowns to limit social contacts and restricting where people could travel.

These restrictions affected everyone including the royal family. Charles did not like to stop working and tried to continue with his schedule of events, but on 13 March 2020, Prince Charles and the Duchess of Cornwall announced the cancellation of a Royal Tour to Bosnia and Herzegovina and the Republic of Cyprus and Jordan. Shortly afterwards, the prince's home, Highgrove House, like many popular attractions, closed to the public to prevent the spread of the virus.

On 23 March 2020, Prime Minister Boris Johnson called on people to help prevent the spread of the virus by staying home, adding that new rules meant people were only allowed to leave their homes to shop for basic necessities, exercise,

Boris Johnson

seek or provide care, or travel to and from work. People were not allowed to meet with friends, or family members they didn't live with. All non-essential workplaces and schools were closed.

In late March 2020, Clarence House announced that Prince Charles had tested positive for the virus and was isolating at Birkhall in Scotland. At seventy-one years old, many worried that Charles might develop a severe form of the disease. They also worried that he may have had contact with the queen, who was at even greater risk.

Thankfully, Charles made a full recovery. Others were not so lucky. Between March 2020 and November 2022, more than 200,000 people in the United Kingdom died within twenty-eight days of becoming infected with the virus.

The virus and the restrictions affected everyone. The lockdowns imposed by the government went on for many months. Many people struggled not being able to see friends and family, others worried about catching the virus or losing their jobs due to the closure of businesses. Children struggled too, missing school and playing with their friends.

William and Catherine gave their support to Public Health England's Every Mind Matters campaign which helped people find ways to protect their mental health and cope with the stress caused by COVID-19 and lockdown.

Charles helped by standing in for the queen at public events. Queen Elizabeth and Prince Philip were isolating at Windsor Castle. Prince Philip's health had been a concern for some time, and at ninety-four years of age, the queen had been advised to protect her health by isolating, too.

My Dear Papa

On 9 April 2021, Charles's father, Prince Philip, Duke of Edinburgh, died at Windsor Castle. Prince Philip had let it be known that he did not want a big funeral. Philip did not like fuss. Charles spoke to his father, shortly before he died, to discuss plans for his one-hundredth birthday party. Prince Philip said, "Well I've got to be alive for it, haven't I?" Prince Philip did not get his one-hundredth birthday party, but he did get a small funeral on 17 April.

Unlike other Royal funerals, which attracted crowds of people to pay their respects,

Charles and Camilla at Prince Philip's funeral

COVID-19 restrictions meant that Prince Philip's was attended by just thirty members of his family and close friends who sat separately and wore masks.

"MY DEAR PAPA WAS A VERY SPECIAL PERSON."

Charles, Prince of Wales

Charles had had a difficult relationship with his father growing up, but as he grew older, Charles and Philip became friends. Charles respected the support Philip had been to his mother, and his sense of duty. They shared a love of fishing and polo and had a similar passion for conservation. Philip was proud of Charles's work to protect the environment.

Charles Declares War

As the world began to open up in 2021, Charles got back to his work. In November, Charles attended the 2021 United Nations Climate Change Conference in Glasgow, also known as COP26. COP26 was a summit that brought world leaders together to work towards meeting targets to combat climate change. In a speech at the opening ceremony of the conference, Charles warned the audience that the devastating effects of climate

Charles giving a speech on Climate Change

change would dwarf COVID-19, and called on people to work together and take a 'war-like footing', to fight it.

"IT IS SURELY TIME TO SET ASIDE OUR DIFFERENCES AND GRASP THIS UNIQUE

OPPORTUNITY TO LAUNCH A SUBSTANTIAL GREEN RECOVERY BY PUTTING THE GLOBAL ECONOMY ON A CONFIDENT, SUSTAINABLE TRAJECTORY AND THUS SAVE OUR PLANET."

Charles, Prince of Wales

While at the conference, Charles spoke to business leaders such as Amazon founder and CEO Jeff Bezos who posted about their meeting:

"WE HAD A CHANCE TO DISCUSS THESE IMPORTANT ISSUES ON THE EVE OF #COP26 - LOOKING FOR SOLUTIONS TO HEAL OUR WORLD, AND HOW THE BEZOSEARTHFUND CAN HELP."

Jeff Bezos

A Witness to Change

Climate change was only one of the many changes that Charles had seen in his lifetime. Another was the change in people's attitudes to monarchy around the world.

At the end of November, Charles travelled to Barbados in the Caribbean to bear witness to this change, attending a ceremony which removed the queen as their head of state and replaced her with their first elected president, Dame Sandra Mason.

Barbados gained independence from the United Kingdom in 1966, but kept the queen as their constitutional monarch. The queen was on their stamps and on their banknotes, and while she didn't have any power, many people felt she was a symbol of a colonial past they wanted to leave behind.

During the ceremony, Charles made a speech expressing his hope for a close relationship between Barbados and United Kingdom in the future but took time to acknowledge the past.

"FROM THE DARKEST DAYS OF OUR PAST, AND THE APPALLING ATROCITY OF SLAVERY, WHICH FOREVER STAINS OUR HISTORY, THE PEOPLE OF THIS ISLAND FORGED THEIR PATH WITH EXTRAORDINARY FORTITUDE."

Charles, Prince of Wales

THE DARKEST DAYS OF OUR PAST

The island of Barbados was first claimed for the British crown in 1625. Like other colonies in the New World, land was allocated to wealthy white settlers. To farm this land, settlers bought enslaved people taken from Africa by traders or human traffickers. Over the next 200 years, more than 380,000 Black Africans were brought to Barbados and sold to white settlers.

The white settlers forced enslaved people to work hard and did not pay them for their labour. When slaves rebelled, they were punished brutally. The work of slaves in Barbados generated vast wealth for the enslavers and their families living in the United Kingdom. Some of this wealth was used to build grand houses and fund universities and museums.

When enslavement was abolished, the British government paid compensation to the slave owners for the loss of their property. The amount of money paid was so vast the government could not pay it all at once; instead they paid in instalments over a number of years. The final instalment was paid in 2015. The people who had been enslaved were not compensated for their labour, or their suffering.

Many in Barbados praised Charles for acknowledging the past, but others didn't think his words went far enough. As slavery took place under the rule of Charles's ancestors, they believed he should apologize, and pay reparations for the unpaid labour of the people of Barbados.

Charles watched as the queen's standard flag was lowered and folded. The ceremony in Barbados was not the first Charles had witnessed, and it would not be the last.

CELEBRATION AND SORROW

The year 2022 was a special year for the royal family because it marked seventy years since Her Majesty Queen Elizabeth came to the throne – her Platinum Jubilee. To mark the occasion, the palace planned a schedule of events spread throughout the year, culminating with a special celebration weekend in June. The events included national and international tours, visits, galas, garden parties, dinners, concerts and parades.

The Jubilee was a celebration, but it was also tinged with sadness. As people gathered, it soon became obvious that somebody very important was missing – Elizabeth herself. Due to concerns for her health, Elizabeth was advised by palace doctors to rest, and she only made short appearances throughout the weekend. Charles and the rest of the family stepped in to make sure the fun went without a hitch, but there was a sense that the reign of Elizabeth II was coming to an end.

A New Queen

With Philip gone, Elizabeth was relying on Charles more than ever. Throughout her reign, Philip had been her partner and a constant source of encouragement and support. Elizabeth wanted to make sure Charles had a similar source of encouragement and support when he took the throne.

When they married, the palace had said that when Charles became king, Camilla would become princess consort. This was because they felt that the role of queen rightly belonged to his first wife, Diana, mother of Princes William and Harry.

But Elizabeth saw how well Camilla and Charles worked as a team. In February 2022, Elizabeth announced that when Charles became king, Camilla would become queen consort and be given the title Queen Camilla. Elizabeth asked that people gave her son and Camilla their support, just as they had to her.

A Family Affair

As part of the Jubilee Celebrations, the palace scheduled a tour of the United Kingdom and countries where Queen Elizabeth was head of state and with which the UK had a strong relationship. As the queen was not able to travel herself, her family stepped in.

In March, Prince Charles and Camilla, Duchess of Cornwall, travelled to the Republic of Ireland. Prince William and Catherine, Duchess of Cambridge, flew to Jamaica and the Bahamas. In May, Charles travelled to Canada with Camilla, Duchess of Cornwall.

Later in May, Charles was asked to take his mother's place in an important occasion that had nothing to do with the Jubilee – the State Opening of Parliament.

Charles gives State Opening of Parliament

THE STATE OPENING OF PARLIAMENT

The State Opening of Parliament marks the beginning of the parliamentary year. As head of state, the monarch is expected to travel to Westminster and dress in special fur-lined robes called the Robes of State. The monarch then sits in the House of Lords, while an official called Black Rod goes to summon the members of the House of Commons. In the United Kingdom, the monarch is forbidden from entering the House of Commons. The door to the House of Commons is slammed in Black Rod's face. Black Rod knocks on the door three times and leads the members of the House to the House of Lords to listen to the monarch give the speech. The speech given by the monarch is written by the government and sets out what they hope to achieve in that parliamentary year.

As well as the Robes of State, the monarch also wears the State Crown. Charles delivered the speech on behalf of his mother, but as he was not the monarch, he could not wear the crown or the Robes of State. Instead, to represent the queen's presence, the Imperial State Crown was carried into the House of Lords on a velvet pillow and placed on a table at Charles's side.

Prince of Party Crashing

As part of the Jubilee Celebrations, Charles and Camilla agreed to appear in a special episode of a television programme on the BBC. But this programme was not a documentary or an interview. Charles had appeared in plenty of those. Instead, it was *Eastenders* – a soap opera set in East London. In the episode, Charles and Camilla appeared to surprise the residents of Albert Square, by showing up at their Jubilee street party and joining them in a toast to the queen.

After a whirlwind of events up and down the country, Jubilee weekend arrived. The queen had had to miss almost all of the parades and concerts, even the Service of Thanksgiving held in her honour at St Paul's Cathedral. Charles attended in her place. Throughout the celebrations, Charles saw how much people loved his mother and wanted to celebrate her. Charles wanted his mother to get the chance to see it, too. On Sunday 5 June, the royal family was scheduled to make an appearance on the balcony at Buckingham Palace. The queen was not feeling well, but Charles thought she should be there. He called his mother and told her about the thousands of people who had travelled to London to celebrate with her and thank her. Charles asked her to try to come if she could. Queen Elizabeth agreed, and Charles walked his mother on to the balcony to greet a crowd that stretched as far as they could see.

After her coronation, Charles and his mother had been on the balcony with his father, his grandmother and Princess Margaret – all of whom were now gone. Seventy years on, Elizabeth and Charles were now surrounded by the future kings and queens. Charles's wife, Camilla; his son, William, and William's wife, Catherine, with their three children, Charles's grandchildren: George, Charlotte and Louis.

Charles stood beside his mother, just as he had done when he was a little boy, after her coronation. The parades of men in uniform, the glittering robes, the horses and carriages: it was all for her, but for the last time. Next time, it would be for him.

Urgent News

At 10.30 am on 8 September, Charles was at Dumfries House when he received a phone call from Balmoral Castle. Charles was needed urgently. Charles cancelled the day's plans, jumped in a helicopter and got there as quickly as he could. Charles was just in time. Elizabeth's doctors had been worried about her for some time, and they were right. At 3.10 pm, the queen died peacefully. Charles and his sister Anne were by her side.

In the United Kingdom, when the sovereign dies, their heir automatically accedes to the throne and becomes king or queen. At 6.30 pm, the news broke on television. Newsreaders in sombre black suits told viewers the queen was dead, and her son Charles was now king.

God Save the King

Charles's full title became His Majesty Charles III, by the Grace of God, of the United Kingdom of Great Britain and Northern Ireland and of His other Realms and Territories King, Head of the Commonwealth, Defender of the Faith.

Charles knew this moment would come from when he was very little. It was the job he was born to do, but it was also a moment he dreaded, because becoming king meant his mother was gone.

"THE DEATH OF MY BELOVED MOTHER, HER MAJESTY THE QUEEN, IS A MOMENT OF THE GREATEST SADNESS FOR ME AND ALL MEMBERS OF MY FAMILY."

King Charles III

But as sad as Charles was, he had work to do …
and that work began right away.

Hitting the Ground Running

After spending the night at Balmoral, King
Charles and Queen Camilla travelled to London.
At Buckingham Palace, people gathered to pay
their respects and leave flowers. When Charles
arrived, he and Camilla stopped to speak with
them. Some offered Charles their condolences,
others said, "God save the king", and one lady
even stole a kiss.

Once inside the palace, Charles's work began.
Charles was now head of state which meant he had
an important role with the government. As head
of state, Charles would have weekly meetings,
called audiences, with the prime minister,
to discuss what was going on in parliament,
the country and the world. Charles met with
Prime Minister Liz Truss that day. Alongside
audiences, Charles would receive a red box from
the government every day, containing details of
what the government was doing and what was

happening in the United Kingdom and around the world. Part of the job of sovereign meant Charles was expected to read these papers every day and sign them, to show he was aware of what they said.

As a constitutional monarch, Charles would be required to remain neutral and not to express his opinion or attempt to influence the running of the government in any way. Some people worried that Charles would struggle to be able to keep his opinions to himself, but Charles knew better than anyone what the role of sovereign required. Charles had grown up watching his mother in the role and had a front row seat for all the challenges she faced in her reign and how she handled them.

The King's Speech

Later that day, Charles made his first address to the nation as its king. In his address, Charles paid tribute to his mother's life of service and dedication to the role of sovereign. Charles promised to do the same.

"AS THE QUEEN HERSELF DID WITH SUCH UNSWERVING DEVOTION, I TOO NOW SOLEMNLY PLEDGE MYSELF, THROUGHOUT THE REMAINING TIME GOD GRANTS ME, TO UPHOLD THE CONSTITUTIONAL PRINCIPLES AT THE HEART OF OUR NATION.

"AND WHEREVER YOU MAY LIVE IN THE UNITED KINGDOM, OR IN THE REALMS AND TERRITORIES ACROSS THE WORLD, AND WHATEVER MAY BE YOUR BACKGROUND OR BELIEFS, I SHALL ENDEAVOUR TO SERVE YOU WITH LOYALTY, RESPECT AND LOVE, AS I HAVE THROUGHOUT MY LIFE."

King Charles III

Charles recognized that, as the king, his life would be very different and that his family's life would be different too. Not only had they lost a beloved mother, grandmother and great-grandmother, they would all now have new roles and responsibilities.

Charles would have many more duties as king, and would no longer be able to spend time working with the charities he cared so much about. This work Charles handed on to other members of the family. Now heir to the throne, William would take on many of the titles that had belonged to his father. Instead of being the Duke and Duchess of Cambridge, William and Catherine would now become the Prince and Princess of Wales. Charles's wife Camilla was now Queen Consort.

The Proclamation

On 10 September, Charles travelled to St James's Palace to attend his proclamation. In the United Kingdom, a new sovereign becomes king or queen the moment the previous sovereign dies.

They are then officially proclaimed sovereign at a meeting of the Accession Council as soon after the death as possible.

The Accession Council is made up of some privy counsellors, great officers of state, the lord mayor and high sheriffs of the City of London, realm high commissioners, some senior civil servants and certain others who are summoned to the Accession Council. The Privy Council includes some cabinet members, the speaker, the leaders of the main political parties, archbishops, various senior judges as well as other senior public figures. Queen Consort Camilla and William, Prince of Wales are also members of the council. At the meeting, the Lord President of the Council – Penny Mordaunt in this case – formally announced the death of Her Majesty the Queen and then read a document called the Accession Proclamation which stated Charles was now king.

King Charles attended the second part of the meeting where he gave his first address to the Privy Council, and signed the Accession Proclamation as well as making an oath promising to preserve the Church of Scotland.

King Charles's proclamation

After the council meeting, the proclamation was read out loud from the proclamation gallery at St James's Palace and other venues around London. Further proclamation ceremonies took place around the United Kingdom. In Cardiff, the proclamation was read in both English and in Welsh, and in Scotland it was read on 11 September in Edinburgh, in both English and Gaelic.

Proclamation ceremonies also took place in the other countries where the king was now head of state. In Canada, Prime Minister Justin Trudeau signed the proclamation following a meeting of Canada's Privy Council Office. In Australia, the proclamation ceremony took place at Parliament House in Canberra. The proclamation was followed by a twenty-one-gun salute and a performance by Indigenous dancers.

Meanwhile, preparations were made for the queen's funeral. From Balmoral, Queen Elizabeth's coffin was taken to the Palace of Holyroodhouse in Edinburgh, before then proceeding to Westminster Hall in London. There it was displayed on a platform called a catafalque where she lay in state. Lying in state is when the coffin of a person who has served the country is displayed in a public building in order for people to come and pay their respects. Hundreds of thousands of people from all over the United Kingdom travelled to London to see her, some queuing for more than twenty-four hours before they entered the hall. For those who were not able to attend, cameras in the hall filmed the queen's coffin and people as they filed past.

On 16 September, King Charles dressed in his military uniform to join his siblings Princess Anne, Prince Andrew and Prince Edward as they stood vigil around their mother's coffin. Later, Elizabeth's eight grandchildren took their turn to pay their respects in this way.

Charles standing vigil at the queen's coffin

A Final Goodbye

The queen's funeral took place three days later. King Charles walked in the funeral procession behind the queen's coffin to Westminster Abbey, alongside his brothers and sister and his sons, Princes William and Harry.

As with Charles's grandfather, King George VI, his mother's funeral was a state funeral, attended by leaders from around the world including United States President Joe Biden, New Zealand Prime Minister Jacinda Ardern, Canadian Prime Minister Justin Trudeau, Japanese Emperor Naruhito, King Letsie III of Lesotho and President Sandra Mason of Barbados. Charles sat right at the front, close to his mother's coffin. A wreath of flowers from Buckingham Palace sat on top of the coffin with a note.

"IN LOVING DEVOTED MEMORY CHARLES R."

After a service at Westminster Abbey, the royal family travelled to Windsor to attend a smaller private ceremony at St George's Chapel, where Charles had to wipe tears from his eyes.

It was an emotional day for Charles, which came after ten of the hardest and busiest days of his life. He'd had barely had a moment to rest since receiving the call from Balmoral. The ten days after the death of Her Majesty Queen Elizabeth II were a chance for the nation to mourn their lost monarch, and Charles worked during each one of them, receiving a red box from the government every day day. The next seven days would be for him. After the funeral, Buckingham Palace released a statement.

"It is His Majesty the King's wish that a period of Royal Mourning be observed from now until seven days after The Queen's Funeral."

Charles travelled to Scotland with Camilla. For Charles, this was a chance to grieve for his "darling Mama". It was also a chance to reflect on all he had achieved as prince, and what life would be like as king.

BUILDING A NEW LEGACY

For most people in the United Kingdom, Queen Elizabeth II was the only monarch they had ever known. The Platinum Jubilee celebrations and the huge number of people who mourned when she died proved that, not only was she well loved, but she was also a tough act to follow.

King Charles and Queen Camilla's first public engagement after the funeral was in Dunfermline, Scotland. There, King Charles III formally confirmed the town's city status, which had been awarded as part of Queen Elizabeth II's Platinum Jubilee celebrations. It was a good start for Charles who was delighted to see so many people there to wish him well, and the visit, which was all smiles and handshakes, was very much like one his mother would have made as queen.

Queen Elizabeth was very rarely seen not

smiling, and people were pleased to see that Charles was able to bring the same joy to a crowd as she had.

Operation Golden Orb

In October 2022, the palace announced that the coronation of King Charles III would take place on 6 May 2023 at Westminster Abbey and be conducted by the archbishop of Canterbury. The plans for the coronation of King Charles were called Operation Golden Orb.

Charles wanted his coronation to reflect his vision of monarchy. He wanted it to include many of the traditional parts of the ceremony, but be shorter so that more people would be able to watch it. Charles also wanted his coronation to be more environmentally friendly. A coronation is a state occasion, which means the government invites leaders and members of royal families from all over the world. More than 8,000 people attended Elizabeth's coronation – so many that special seats had to be installed inside Westminster Abbey. Charles did not want so many people flying in for his ceremony; instead he wanted just 2,000, as many as the Abbey could hold without being altered.

Charles believed his coronation should be cheaper, too, as he didn't think it was appropriate for the government to spend a large amount of money on a coronation when many people in the United Kingdom were struggling to afford food and to heat their homes.

BRITAIN IN 2022

As well as having a tough act to follow, Charles became king at a difficult time for the country and the commonwealth. Charles inherited a kingdom that was far from united.

BREXIT

In 2016, the British government asked people to vote in a special election called a referendum. They wanted people to decide whether Great Britain should remain part of an organization called the European Union. The European Union (it had previously been known as the EEC, which was formed in 1957) was formed in 1993 to bring member countries together to make decisions about trade, human rights, the environment and security that benefited the people living there.

Some people in Britain believed that being a member of the EU meant that decisions about issues that affected the UK were decided not by the elected members of the British government, but by the European Parliament that was made up of members that were not elected by the British public. These people believed that people in the United Kingdom would be better off if the UK left the European Union.

The majority of people who voted, voted to leave the EU – although the vote was extremely close. Leaving the EU affected trade with countries in

Europe, and also meant that many people from EU countries who had been living and working in the UK had to leave and some people in Britain had to leave their homes in Europe.

THE PANDEMIC

The COVID-19 pandemic caused many problems in the United Kingdom. In order to stop the spread of the virus the government implemented lockdowns. Lockdowns stopped people from leaving their homes to go to work and this forced many businesses to close. Some businesses managed to survive, but others failed.

Due to economic problems caused by Brexit and the pandemic, the British pound wasn't worth as much as before, which meant buying food and fuel from abroad was very expensive. The price of food in shops and people's gas and electricity bills increased dramatically, whereas their wages or the amount of money they received in benefits from the government stayed the same. This caused many people to struggle to afford things that they had been able to afford before and made it difficult for them to pay their bills and buy food.

THE WAR IN UKRAINE

On 24 April 2022, Russian President Vladimir Putin ordered his troops at the Ukrainian border to launch an attack on Ukraine. President Putin launched the attack because he did not want Ukraine to form alliances with countries that he saw as a threat to Russia.

From 1922 to 1991, Russia and Ukraine, as well as several other countries such as Lithuania and Belarus, were part of a large group of countries called the Union of Soviet Socialist Republics or USSR. After the Soviet Union collapsed in 1991, these countries became independent, formed their own governments and relationships with other countries around the world. President Vladimir Putin did not like these countries forming alliances. In particular, Putin did not want countries like Ukraine joining an alliance called the North Atlantic Treaty Organization (NATO). NATO is made up of countries in North America and Europe whose leaders signed an agreement to protect one another should they be attacked.

HOW THIS AFFECTED THE UNITED KINGDOM

Although not yet a member of NATO, after Ukraine was attacked, other countries offered their support by sending arms to help the Ukrainian forces fight the Russians, pledging aid and implementing sanctions against Russia. Sanctions are a kind of political punishment designed to hurt the economy of a country they are imposed on. These sanctions included banning the import of Russian goods.

In response to these sanctions, Vladimir Putin ordered the Russian gas industry to stop supplying as much gas to Europe. Gas is used to fuel power stations to produce electricity and to heat people's homes. Before the war in Ukraine, Russia supplied 40 per cent of the gas used in Europe. Cutting the supply caused the price of gas in Europe and the United Kingdom to increase, and people's bills to rise further.

The rise in bills also affected businesses, which meant they had to raise their prices to cover the cost. Almost everything became more expensive than it was the year before and yet people were earning the same amount of money. People who were struggling before could no longer afford to pay their rent, buy food and pay their bills.

Although Charles wanted his coronation to be different to his mother's, he wanted some parts to stay the same.

Like the coronation of Queen Elizabeth II and the kings and queens before her, Charles's coronation will take place as follows.

The Recognition

The archbishop calls for people to recognize Charles as their undoubted king. The congregation responds by saying, "God save the king!"

The Oath

The archbishop will then ask Charles to swear the coronation oath.

The Anointing

During the anointing Charles is led to the coronation chair and a golden canopy is held over his head. The archbishop then marks Charles with a cross on his head, hands and heart using holy oil.

The Investiture

During the investiture, Charles is given the same coronation regalia given to his mother (see page 68), before being crowned with the St Edward's Crown.

Enthronement and Homage

For the enthronement, Charles walks from the coronation chair to the throne where the archbishop and Charles's heirs, including William, kneel before him and promise to serve him, just as Charles did to his mother when he was invested as Prince of Wales (see page 113).

Like his mother's coronation, and unlike the coronations of the kings and queens before her, Charles's ceremony will also be televised and streamed around the world.

A Controversial Crown

As queen consort, Camilla will be anointed and crowned in a shorter ceremony after Charles.

Camilla's crown will be the one used by King Charles's grandmother, queen consort to King George VI. This crown is known as the Queen Mother's Crown. The Queen Mother's Crown is made of platinum and contains a famous and controversial gemstone – the Koh-I-Noor diamond.

A Stone with a Story

The Koh-i-Noor diamond is part of the Queen Mother's Crown because this crown is only ever worn by women. According to an ancient Hindu legend the Koh-I-Noor brings bad luck to any man who wears it.

"ONLY GOD OR WOMAN CAN WEAR IT WITH IMPUNITY."

Hindu legend

The Koh-I-Noor diamond was given to Queen Victoria by the East India Company, who claimed to have been given it by the maharaja, or great king, of Punjab when they annexed his territory.

THE EAST INDIA COMPANY

In 1600, Queen Elizabeth I granted an organization named the East India Company exclusive trade rights over territory in the Indian Ocean. As well as trade rights, she also granted the company the right to govern, or rule, on behalf of the British crown. The East India Company wanted to control the area because it was rich in spices, fine cotton, silk, precious metals and gemstones. But they weren't the only people who wanted to control this trade. In order for the East India Company to control it, they needed to be able to fight other interested parties.

As the East India Company took control of the Indian subcontinent, they built factories to manufacture goods that made a lot of money. When Muslim, Sikh and Hindu people who lived in the region objected or protested against the East India Company's governors or laws, the East India Company went to war against them with their own army. As their wealth grew, they took control of more territory and built fortifications to defend themselves.

In the 1840s, the East India Company set their sights on an area in the northeast of the subcontinent known as Punjab, which means "five rivers". Punjab was ruled by a Sikh maharajah, or great king, named Ranjit Singh, who wore the glittering Koh-I-Noor on his arm. Ranjit Singh was known as the Lion of Punjab because he was a great leader with a powerful army. When Ranjit Singh died in 1839, his throne and the diamond passed to his sons. Having wanted the territory for some time, the East India Company saw the death of Ranjit as an opportunity to take it. Over the next five years, the company fought fierce battles against Punjab in two Anglo-Sikh wars.

After Ranjit Singh's death, the throne of Punjab changed hands four times as each of his sons died horrible deaths. In 1843, the throne passed to Ranjit Singh's youngest son, Duleep Singh, who was just five years old. Duleep's mother, Rani Jindan, ruled in his place. The East India Company saw this as their chance, and attacked. When Duleep and his mother did not surrender their territory, the East India Company kidnapped Queen Rani and locked her away. Without his mother to guide him, and afraid for her life, ten-year-old Duleep had no choice but to sign his kingdom, and the Koh-I-Noor diamond, over to the East India Company.

The East India Company shipped the stone to the United Kingdom. When it arrived, people were disappointed with it. Though it was large, it was not as brilliant as people expected it to be. Queen Victoria's husband, Prince Albert, had the stone recut to make it more sparkly. The original 191-carat stone was cut to 105 carats. Queen Victoria wore the diamond as a brooch.

After her death, King Edward VII had the stone mounted in the crown used to crown his wife, Queen Alexandra, and it has remained within the crown ever since.

Many people believe the stone should be returned to India because of the way it was taken and because it is a symbol of the wealth the British stole from the region. A representative for the Indian government said that the use of the diamond as part of the coronation would bring back, "painful memories of a colonial past".

The Monarchy of the Future

At seventy-three years of age, Charles's reign is likely to be shorter than his mother's. Charles very much wanted to continue her work, while also bringing the monarchy into the twenty-first century and preparing it for the future reign of his son, William, and his grandson George.

Throughout his time as Prince of Wales, Charles said that he wanted to modernize the monarchy and make it more relevant to the people today. His ideas included reducing the number of people who were working royals, opening up palaces to the public, and making the monarchy more affordable.

"SOMETHING AS CURIOUS AS THE MONARCHY WON'T SURVIVE UNLESS YOU TAKE ACCOUNT OF PEOPLE'S ATTITUDES. AFTER ALL, IF PEOPLE DON'T WANT IT, THEY WON'T HAVE IT."

King Charles III as Prince of Wales

And attitudes to monarchy were very different to when his mother came to the throne, both in the United Kingdom and around the world.

In November 2022, King Charles was in York to unveil a statue of his late mother, the queen. As Charles was shaking hands with people who had come to see him, a protestor shouted that Charles was not his king and that the United Kingdom was built on the "blood of slaves". The protestor threw eggs at Charles, before being arrested.

Some in the crowd shouted "God save the king", but while they may not have shared the protestor's view, others in the country, and other countries where Charles was now head of state, did.

Acknowledging the Past

For some people, the king and the royal family are a cause for celebration and a symbol of the rich history of the United Kingdom. For other people around the world, the royal family represents a painful legacy of slavery, colonialism and white privilege.

Charles acceded the throne not long after

a royal tour where countries such as Belize, Jamaica, the Bahamas and Canada made their feelings about his legacy very clear.

Jamaican Flag

In March 2022, Prince William and the Duchess of Cambridge had visited Belize and Jamaica as part of the Platinum Jubilee tour. The purpose of the visit was to strengthen ties with members of the commonwealth. The tour did not go to plan. In Belize, local people protested their arrival, and in Jamaica their visit was overshadowed by the Jamaican government announcing their plan to remove the queen as head of state and a government committee in the Bahamas signing a letter asking them to apologize for slavery and for the UK to pay reparations.

"I FEEL AS IF MORE
YOUNGER PEOPLE
ARE AWARE OF THE
WRONGDOINGS OF THE
MONARCHY. THE OLDER
GENERATIONS IN BELIZE
GREW UP BRITISH, AND
HAD A LOYALTY TO THE
CROWN. A LOT OF US
GREW UP WITH THAT
MINDSET BEING PASSED

DOWN TO US, BUT I THINK WITH PLATFORMS SUCH AS TIKTOK AND YOUTUBE, THE YOUNG PEOPLE OF BELIZE ARE GAINING ACCESS TO MORE EDUCATION SURROUNDING OUR COUNTRY'S COLONIAL HISTORY."

Jelissa, 25 – Belize

THE ROYAL FAMILY AND ENSLAVEMENT

While King Charles III was born long after slavery was abolished, some people believe he should apologize to the descendants of enslaved people. This is because Charles is the head of a family or organization who played a big part in, and profited from, the trade in enslaved African people from the reign of Queen Elizabeth I until it was abolished. In 1672, Charles's namesake, King Charles II, granted a royal charter to the Royal African Company, giving it permission to buy, sell and transport African people to North America and the Caribbean. The people transported by the Royal African Company were branded with hot irons with the coat of arms of the company's initials. The sovereign and the government of the United Kingdom protected, and profited from, the slave trade until it was abolished by an act of parliament in 1807, and enslavement in fact continued within the British Empire until 1833.

Charles addressed this history at the annual commonwealth conference in Rwanda in 2022, where he said that the roots of the commonwealth:

"ASSOCIATION RUN DEEP INTO THE MOST PAINFUL PERIOD OF OUR HISTORY. I CANNOT DESCRIBE THE DEPTHS OF MY PERSONAL SORROW AT THE SUFFERING OF SO MANY, AS I CONTINUE TO DEEPEN MY OWN

UNDERSTANDING OF SLAVERY'S ENDURING IMPACT. IF WE ARE TO FORGE A COMMON FUTURE THAT BENEFITS ALL OUR CITIZENS, WE TOO MUST FIND NEW WAYS TO ACKNOWLEDGE OUR PAST."

King Charles III as Prince of Wales

Many people did not think Charles's statement went far enough and hoped as king he would say more.

Truth and Reconciliation

• •

In May 2022, Charles and Camilla visited Canada also as part of the Platinum Jubilee tour. The leaders of the First Nations and Métis National Council asked Charles and Queen Elizabeth to take part in a solemn reflection and prayer to acknowledge the part the Anglican Church, and the Canadian government, played in the running of residential schools for Indigenous children.

RESIDENTIAL SCHOOLS

From the 1500s, ships filled with people, known as settlers, sailed from England to North America. When they arrived, the settlers seized land, on behalf of the English crown, from the Indigenous peoples who had lived there for thousands of years. As well as land, the settlers took resources such as food and timber. To prevent Indigenous people from taking back their land, the settlers attacked them, and attempted to destroy the culture of those who survived. They did this by imposing English law, and religion, and by making many aspects of Indigenous culture illegal. The settlers forced the Indigenous peoples to live on areas of land known as reservations. Despite all of this, Indigenous people persevered and did everything they could to preserve their culture. To stop this, the English on behalf of the crown, set up residential schools to educate Indigenous children. Similar schools were set up in Australia and New Zealand.

From the late nineteenth century until 1970, the Anglican Church ran schools in Canada for Indigenous pupils who had been taken away from their families by force. These schools were part of a plan to systematically destroy Indigenous culture by removing children from their families and separating them from their language, their history and their traditions.

Instead, these children were taught to follow the Anglican Church and obey the queen. Classes were taught in English and children were often punished for speaking in the language of their parents. Children taken to these schools often did not see their families for many years and some never saw their families again. Punishments were harsh and many children were abused. Thousands of children died in these schools and were buried in unmarked graves.

As sovereign, the queen was head of the Anglican Church and head of state for Canada, for part of this time. In Canada, the survivors of residential schools campaigned for many years for acknowledgement of what was done to them and for compensation from the Canadian government for the pain they suffered. Their campaigning resulted in an agreement with the Canadian government and a formal process of reconciliation. In Canada, 30 September is National Day for Truth and Reconciliation where people are encouraged to wear orange in support of survivors of residential schools, and in memory of the children who never came home.

In May 2022, the archbishop of Canterbury apologized on behalf of the Anglican Church, and in July 2022, Pope Francis apologized for damage done to the Indigenous people of Canada by the Catholic Church.

While in Canada, Charles met with leaders of the Indigenous peoples of Canada and expressed his sorrow for the families of the children found in unmarked graves, but he did not go as far as to apologize on behalf of the royal family.

"I WANT TO ACKNOWLEDGE THEIR SUFFERING AND TO SAY HOW MUCH OUR HEARTS GO OUT TO THEM AND THEIR FAMILIES."

Charles, Prince of Wales 2022

As Prince, Charles travelled to many countries and spoke with leaders, including presidents and prime ministers, as well as community and Indigenous leaders. Charles listened to what they told him and was aware that if he wanted to take the monarchy into the future, he had to acknowledge the negative feelings many people had about its past.

A Tour Fit for a King

After his coronation, Charles plans to go on a tour of more than fifty-two commonwealth countries including Australia and New Zealand, as well as many other countries with which the United Kingdom has good relations. Charles is also expected to visit European countries in order to help build relationships after Brexit.

King Charles hopes that the tour will help rebuild and strengthen the United Kingdom's relationships with countries where he is head of state, within the commonwealth and beyond, and ensure his legacy as king will be one his heirs are proud to take with them into the next century.

ABOUT THE AUTHOR

Sally Morgan was born in Malaysia but grew up in England. She studied Literature and Classics at university. After graduating, she worked as a bookseller and as an editor before becoming a full-time writer. She is the author of many books including *Dream Big* and the *My Best Friend* series. Sally lives in Minneapolis, USA, with her husband and two children.

GLOSSARY

Abdication – an act completed by the reigning monarch, where they formally give up their powers as a monarch.

Activist – a person who campaigns to bring attention and bring about political or social change.

Apartheid – a government policy in South Africa that instituted segregation (separation) between white and Black people. The policy lasted from 1948 to 1994.

Climate change – changes in the long-term average weather (or climate) of a single place (regional) or the whole world (global). Climate change refers to the process of the climate changing at faster rates than it would naturally change.

Colony – a place under the political control of another country.

Commonwealth of Nations – an international association which includes the UK and countries that used to be part of the British empire. Other countries are also able to join.

Conservationist – a person who tries to preserve and protect the environment from human activity that is causing the destruction of Earth's habitats.

Coronation – the ceremony crowning a monarch.

Covid-19 – a family of viruses that often affects animals, but sometimes moves from animals to humans. COVID–19 is a new virus that affects humans.

Deforestation – the act of clearing a wide expanse of trees. When talking about deforestation it is in regards to the decrease in forest size in habitats around the world, which many animal species need to thrive.

Election – the formal process by which people vote to choose a person or group of people to an official position in government.

Empire – a group of people or countries ruled over by one person (called the emperor or empress) or government.

Endangered species – animal species that are in danger of dying out or becoming extinct.

First World War – taking place between 1914–1918, this was a global conflict that was fought in Europe and involved many countries around the world, including countries in Africa, Asia and the Middle East.

Global warming – the long-term warming of Earth's overall temperature.

Governess – an out-dated term referring to a private tutor.

Government – made up of a group of people that have the authority to rule a country.

Heir – a person that will legally inherit the property or rank of another person on that person's death.

House of Lords – the second group of government officials in the UK parliament. They are independent from the House of Commons but they share responsibility for creating laws and overseeing the work of the government.

Investiture – a ceremony where the monarch invests honours or rank on a specific person.

Monarchy – a type of government which recognizes a king or queen as head of state, even though they may not hold any political power.

Pandemic – a sudden and widespread outbreak of an infectious disease.

Parliament – the part of government that has the power to make laws. Parliament also oversees the work of the government and represents the general public.

Patron – someone who provides support to a person, organization or cause.

Pollution – the introduction of poisonous or harmful materials into the environment. Pollution can be chemicals, but also noise, light and sound. These can disrupt how ecosystems work and harm the animals and plants within them.

Prime minister – the head of an elected government.

Proclamation – an announcement made by a public official about something important, such as a new monarch.

Queen consort – The wife of a currently reigning king.

Rations – the fixed amount of a commodity officially allocated to each person during times of shortage, such as wartime.

Realm – an old-fashioned term referring to a kingdom.

Reign – period of time when each monarch ruled.

Second World War – a global conflict between two groups of countries, the Allies and the Axis powers.

Sovereign – the ruler or head of state or country.

INDEX

QUEEN ELIZABETH II

It will be for us... to make the world of tomorrow a better and happier place.

A LiFe STORY

1926 - 2022

DAVID ATTENBOROUGH

CHERISH the NATURAL WORLD, because YOU'RE a PART of it ...AND you DEPEND on it.

A LiFe STORY

Natural Historian

CAPTAIN TOM MOORE

The sun will shine on you again and the clouds will go away.

A LiFe STORY

World War Two veteran and fundraiser

STEPHEN HAWKING

Without IMPERFECTION neither YOU nor I would EXIST.

A LiFe STORY

Theoretical Physicist

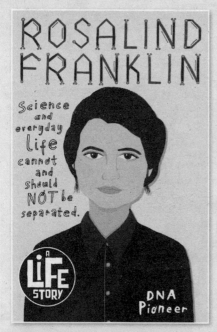

ROSALIND FRANKLIN

Science and everyday **life** cannot and should **NOT** be separated.

A **LIFE** STORY

DNA Pioneer

KAMALA HARRIS

What I want young women and girls to know is:

you are powerful and your voice matters.

A **LIFE** STORY

Vice President

ALAN TURING

I propose to consider the question,

'Can machines think?'

A **LIFE** STORY

Computer Scientist

KATHERINE JOHNSON

There will always be SCIENCE, ENGINEERING and TECHNOLOGY

And there will always, always be MATHEMATICS

A **LIFE** STORY

NASA Mathematician

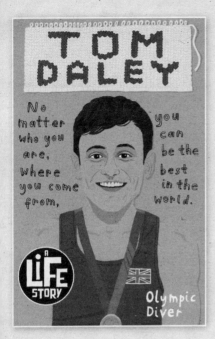

TOM DALEY

No matter who you are, where you come from, you can be the best in the world.

A LiFe Story

🇬🇧 Olympic Diver

SERENA WILLIAMS

WHATEVER fear I have INSIDE me, my DESIRE to WIN is always STRONGER.

A LiFe Story

Tennis Player

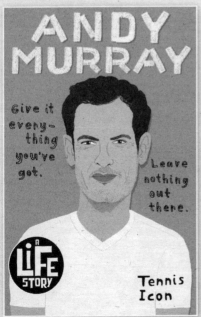

ANDY MURRAY

Give it every-thing you've got.

Leave nothing out there.

A LiFe Story

Tennis Icon

EMMA RADUCANU

Playing sport, and having to be bold on the court and fearless and fight, it's given me inner strength.

A LiFe Story

Tennis Superstar